Christmas Is Not Your Birthday

15TH ANNIVERSARY EDITION

Christmas Is Not Your Birthday
Experiencing the Joy of Living
and Giving Like Jesus
15th Anniversary Edition

Christmas Is Not Your Birthday
978-1-7910-4593-7
978-1-7910-4594-4 *eBook*

Christmas Is Not Your Birthday DVD
978-1-7910-4595-1

Cover description: The cover features a deep red background with the title *Christmas Is Not Your Birthday* in large gold lettering. At the top, white text reads "15th Anniversary Edition," with "Foreword by Rachel Billups" below. An open white gift box tied with a red ribbon reveals a small nativity scene with Mary, Joseph, and the baby Jesus beneath a stable. Beneath the image, the subtitle reads, *Experience the Joy of Living and Giving Like Jesus*. The author's name, Mike Slaughter, appears in large white text at the bottom.

15TH ANNIVERSARY EDITION

Foreword by Rachel Billups

Christmas Is Not Your Birthday

Experience the Joy of Living and Giving Like Jesus

Mike Slaughter

Abingdon Press | Nashville

Christmas Is Not Your Birthday
Experience the Joy of Living and Giving Like Jesus
15th Anniversary Edition

The first edition of this book (ISBN 978-1-4267-2735-1) can be found under Library of Congress Control Number 2011012163.

978-1-7910-4593-7

MANUFACTURED IN THE UNITED STATES OF AMERICA

In honor of our
twin granddaughters,
Kate Sarah Slaughter
and
Zoey Lynn Slaughter

CONTENTS

WATCH YOUR STUDY ANYTIME, ANYWHERE.

Access your *A Different Kind of Christmas* videos and leader resources on any device with your Amplify Media account.

Get Started In Two Steps

1 Scan the QR code or go to My.AmplifyMedia.com /amplify/redeem

2 Create your free account and enter your companion code

Companion Code
MSTWOCFC

Once You're In

- Videos and leader resources saved to your account
- Watch anytime on phone, tablet, or TV
- Come back anytime at My.AmplifyMedia.com

Keep Track of Your Log In Info

Email ______________________________

Password ______________________________

Companion code subject to expiration. Code may be redeemed only by the recipient of this book. Code may not be transferred or sold separately. Internet connection required.

AMPLIFY™ MEDIA

FOREWORD

There is a moment every year, right around the first week of November, when the world seems to shift. The air changes. The stores fill with red and green. The lists begin. The expectations quietly stack on top of one another. And before we know it, we are caught in a current so strong that it carries us straight through December without ever stopping to ask the most important question: What is all of this for?

I know this current all too well. I am a mother, a wife, and a pastor, and I am just as susceptible to the pull of the holiday machine as anyone. I love giving gifts. I love the sparkle and the music and the gathering of people I love around a table. I am not immune to the intoxicating energy of the season, and that is exactly why I need this book.

Mike Slaughter has been my mentor for more than twenty years, and if there is one thing I have learned from walking alongside him, it is that he will always tell you the truth. It's not going to be the easy or comfortable truth, but rather Mike's brand of truth is gut-honest and Spirit-led. It's the kind of truth that makes you sit up a little straighter and rethink assumptions you did not even realize you were carrying.

Mike Slaughter is authentically and terribly human. He has never pretended to have it all figured out. He would be the first to tell you that he, too, needs the reminder that Christmas is not his birthday. And I think that is what makes this book so powerful. It is not written from a place of perfection. It is written from lived experience, from the life of a pastor and a disciple, from someone who has spent decades wrestling with what it means to follow Jesus in a culture that would rather we just keep shopping. He likes his stuff, and he will tell you that the struggle is real! So as you begin reading these pages, recognize that this is someone who is wrestling with consumerism right out loud.

Christmas Is Not Your Birthday changed the way I understand the season. Before I encountered this book, I understood Christmas the way most American Christians do. It was a time of celebration, yes, but also a time of accumulation. What's another gift? Of course, I can add an additional event to the calendar, and the more obligations, the merrier! This book reframes the season and invites us to reimagine Christmas and the season of Advent. Mike's invitation cuts through all that noise like a prophetic word spoken directly into the chaos of my December calendar. He asks a question I had never really sat with before: What if Christmas is not about us at all? That question rearranged something in me. It still does every time I return to this book—because the answer Mike offers is not guilt or shame; his answer is the Incarnation itself. God chose to become flesh and blood and move into the neighborhood. The creator of the universe looked at a broken, aching, beautiful world and said, *I am coming to you*. Jesus wasn't born with a gift registry, not with a wish list, but with a boundary-crossing, breathtaking love that showed up in the most unlikely of places. This baby showed up at a feeding trough, born to a peasant family in a forgotten corner of the Roman Empire.

The Incarnation is more than a sweet story we tell ourselves once a year. It is God breaking into our lives in a way that changes everything. And if we really believe that, if we really believe that the Word became flesh and dwelt among us, then the way we celebrate that reality ought to reflect that belief. That is the invitation Mike extends in these pages. Mike isn't asking us to cancel Christmas. He's not even suggesting that we strip away every tradition, but rather that we reorient the whole season around the one whose birthday we are celebrating.

I've experienced firsthand what it looks like to accept this invitation, because I had the privilege of engaging in ministry for eight years at Ginghamsburg Church. I can tell you this: Christmas hits different at Ginghamsburg. Ginghamsburg is a primarily blue-collar, working-class congregation in the Dayton, Ohio area, and for decades, they have practiced something extraordinary every Christmas Eve. Instead of turning inward toward themselves and their families, they choose to turn outward toward their neighbors. Every dollar given on Christmas Eve goes outside the walls of the church—every single dollar. They call it the Christmas Miracle Offering, and it is exactly what it sounds like. It's a congregation choosing, year after year, to celebrate Jesus's birthday by giving generously toward the needs that break God's heart. The invitation was always the same: Bring a gift to Jesus equal to or greater than what you spend on your own family. Reader, let that settle in for a moment—equal to or greater. It certainly was never a comfortable ask, but it was always a holy one.

What inspired me, year after year, was the people's generosity. These were not wealthy donors giving from surplus. These were working families—factory workers, teachers, people stretching every paycheck. These were children saving up their allowance money to ensure that their peers in other parts of the world had clean drinking water. And yet every Christmas Eve, they showed up with a kind of sacrificial generosity that made you catch your breath.

They gave not because they had extra but because they believed that celebrating the birth of Jesus meant actually living like Jesus is alive, right here, right now, incarnate! They believed the offering was not something tacked on to the end of a service. It was worship itself. I remember the year the leadership team asked a question that I believe every church should ask as they approach the Christmas season: God, what is happening in our community that breaks your heart?

In 2019, the Miami Valley was devastated by fifteen tornadoes, a mass shooting, the ongoing opioid crisis, and a significant decline in community health. The needs that Christmas season were not abstract: These were our neighbors, these were our families, and these were our children. Ginghamsburg responded, and the entire Christmas Eve offering went outside the walls. It supported longtime partners already doing the work of recovery and restoration. And then God revealed something more. There was a growing need in parts of Dayton for access to healthy food. In parts of the community, families had little access to fresh fruits, vegetables, or meats. For many, the only options were dollar stores and convenience stores. This was not just about hunger. It was about health. It was about dignity. So Ginghamsburg partnered with Homefull and other local organizations, including Dayton Children's Hospital, Montgomery County, Premier Health, and Kettering Health, to help launch a mobile grocery store. Together, we were able to bring affordable, healthy food into communities that needed it. The goal was to have a lasting impact and increase the health and well-being of families across the region. I'll never forget standing in that mobile grocery store with a church logo on its side and thinking to myself, *this is what it means to love Jesus and do something about it.*

This is what happens when a church takes the Incarnation seriously. This is what happens when Christmas is not your birthday. That is what happens when the body of Christ moves toward the pain of the world instead of away from it. Ginghamsburg has a long history of sharing sacrificially at Christmastime in tangible and surprising ways. And it all flows from a simple conviction: The God who came to us in Jesus is still coming. God is still moving and still calling ordinary people to participate in extraordinary acts of love.

Mike has always been honest about who he is and who he is not. He has never claimed to be the most likely candidate for leading a movement, but that is exactly the point. God has a history of choosing unlikely people to do extraordinary things.

I have witnessed Mike follow the Holy Spirit into places he would not naturally go. I have watched him wrestle, question, grow, and change. I have watched him model a kind of faith that does not settle for practicing comfortable religion but insists on being transformed by the living Christ. And I have watched a congregation follow that kind of leadership not into ease but into mission. I believe that is what a mentor does. A mentor doesn't just teach you what to think; they show you how to live.

This is the Wesleyan way. Personal piety and social holiness are not competing values. They belong together. You cannot truly love God without loving your neighbor, and you cannot truly love your neighbor without being rooted in the love of God. This book is an invitation to reevaluate not merely our consumerism but our consumption. This is the invitation to rethink not just what we buy but what we worship. Today, we have the opportunity not just in how we spend our money but also in how we spend our attention, our time, and our love.

Spending less and consuming less is not deprivation. It is a breath of fresh air. It is freedom. It is the kind of holy disruption that makes room for the Holy Spirit to move in ways we never expected. As I read these pages, I keep returning to one simple and revolutionary idea: Christmas is a missional opportunity to love our neighbors on purpose. It is so easy to get swept up in the hustle and miss the whole thing. But what if this season could be different? What if, instead of exhausting ourselves in a performance of generosity, we leaned into a Christ who came near? What if we asked God to show us what breaks the divine heart and then actually responded?

I must be honest; I deeply need this invitation every single year. The pull of the culture is strong. The messages are loud. And every November, I must decide again whether I will be carried along or whether I will stand in the story of a God who loved the world enough to step into it.

This book is a gift. Of course, it's not a gift wrapped in paper but one wrapped in truth and grace. It is the gift of perspective. It is a reminder that we can do better, that we can be better, that when the body of Christ moves together, we can do, as Jesus said, "greater things than these" (John 14:12).

I have seen it. I have been part of it, and I am continuing to be shaped by it.

Here is my invitation to you as you begin. Let this book mess with your Christmas. Let it rearrange your priorities. Let it challenge what you think this season is for and who this season is all about, and then offer yourself, your calendar, and your bank account to God. Ask God to open your eyes and your energy to your neighbors near and far. And then bring an offering not just for the people you know but for the neighbors you have not yet met. Bring a gift for the communities that are crying out and for the world that God so loved. The best way to celebrate the birth of Jesus is to live like he is alive. Reader, Christmas is not your birthday; that honor belongs to Jesus.

—Rachel Billups

INTRODUCTION

CHRISTMAS IS NOT YOUR BIRTHDAY!

It is October 12, and I am on my way to the local mall to purchase a new carry-on bag. The wheels on the one I have been using for the last eight years are worn out. I am scanning the satellite radio channels and notice that one station has already switched to a twenty-four-hour Christmas music format. Bruce Springsteen is singing familiar reminders about Santa Claus seeing you "when you're sleeping" and knowing "when you're awake."

My mother used such reminders as part of some behavioral modification strategy leading up to the Christmas season every year. She knew how much we kids anticipated the Sears and Roebuck Christmas catalog each September (decades ago, when we still had Christmas catalogs). Children of my generation, the baby boomers, would study its toy pages daily, like racetrack junkies studying betting odds, circling and prioritizing the desired commodities in hopes of a Christmas Day payoff.

Christmas was like a second birthday but a much bigger and better deal! Mom's reminder was clear: I'd better be good, or I would get a lump of coal in my stocking instead of the new Red Ryder BB gun that I was willing to trade my little sister for. (Apparently, the reminders worked, because I did get my Red Ryder that Christmas. No, I didn't shoot my eye out, but I did ricochet a BB off my forehead once while target shooting in our basement.)

As we grow older, our desired gifts become more sophisticated. Playskool toys no longer suffice; now the demand is for the expensive "new, slimmer" PlayStation 5 or the latest iPhone. Unfortunately, the idolatrous promise of the desired object to bring us life fulfillment and meaning is never realized. The newness eventually wears off, and we seek the next new, best thing. We are hypnotically lured by the seductive marketing sirens of mindless consumption: "You have the power to make the gamer on your list very merry this holiday season with a cool new flat-screen console—the best gift of the season!" By buying into these false promises of secular consumerism, however, we continue to feed our children's materialistic, self-focused addictions.

I arrive at the mall and notice that the marketing preparations are in full swing. Santa Land is under construction with workers on motorized lifts hanging banners heralding the season of conspicuous consumption.

According to the National Retail Federation, in 2025, adult consumers planned to spend an average of $890 on holiday food, decorations, and presents. In a two-parent family, that equates to roughly $1,780.[1] Now, add this cost to the average American household credit card balance of $10,700, with an annual average interest rate over 20 percent.[2]

Christmas has been hijacked and exploited. We have professed allegiance to Jesus but celebrate his birth with an avalanche of materialism.

Christmas is not your birthday; it's Jesus's birthday! This study will help you reclaim the broader missional meaning of Jesus's birth and experience a Christmas season with more peace and joy than any toy or gadget could ever bring.

Chapter 1

EXPECT A MIRACLE

Chapter 1

EXPECT A MIRACLE

Therefore the Lord himself will give you a sign: The virgin will conceive and give birth to a son, and will call him Immanuel.

(Isaiah 7:14)

What does God look like? How would you recognize God if or when God showed up?

Many artists have attempted to depict God's image in countless ways throughout the millennia, whereas others have deemed it blasphemous to do so. Centuries before Jesus's birth, the ancient prophets spoke of the coming of a messiah deliverer, who would be called:

> *Wonderful Counselor, Mighty God,*
> *Everlasting Father, Prince of Peace.*
> *Of the greatness of his government and peace*
> *there will be no end.*
>
> *(Isaiah 9:6-7)*

But this messiah king would also know suffering and rejection (Isaiah 53). His mission would clearly prioritize the poor and the marginalized (Isaiah 61:1-8).

Expectations of what this messiah would be like and look like, however, were quite diverse and even contradictory. Some expected a worldly political revolutionary who would restore the glory days of the Davidic kingdom, whereas others visualized a messiah who represented the Greek ideal of focusing totally on the afterlife.

What is your mental picture of God when you pray? A critical, condemning judge or a merciful, loving parent? A God who favors some over others or a God who loves all creation and all people who make up this incredible planet? Do you picture a savior who is concerned only with saving people for life after death or one who is actively engaged in restoring and renewing devastated places? Do you believe that God always rewards obedience with material wealth and physical health or that God remains present with us in poverty, pain, and suffering?

Jesus was not what most folks expected. When you think about God, adjectives like *powerful*, *majestic*, and *almighty* tend to come to mind. But Jesus did not come to the earth with any air of worldly wealth or majestic power. On the contrary, everything about Jesus's life stood in stark contrast to worldly priorities and values. He arrived on the scene not in strength but in weakness. He was born a Jew into a community of marginalized, oppressed people, spending his early years as a refugee in Egypt. His formative years were spent in a nondescript village, as a member of an ordinary working-class family.

As a man, he lived in tension with the organized religious system. He resisted the world's obsessions with wealth, pleasure, power, and recognition. He identified with the weak and powerless, the widow and the orphan. He did not condemn but defended the sinner. So what does God look like? Like Jesus! Jesus was the embodiment of God's values and priorities. He is Immanuel, "God with us." In Jesus, we see not only the face of God but also the fullness of his humanity, which you and I are created to be. I can believe in a God who looks like Jesus!

Santa Claus Jesus

Too often, however, we view God like Santa Claus—a genie in a bottle, here to fulfill three wishes. All we have to do is name it and claim it, believe it and receive it! We have created this Santa Claus Jesus in our own image, a golden-calf messiah who promises to fulfill all our earthly wants and wishes, an idol of consumption who supports the human quest for meaning and purpose in material things outside of the demands of the earthly historical Jesus who calls us to die to ourselves, to take up our crosses, to sell our possessions and follow him. Jesus always challenged people who wanted to follow him to count the cost.

"As they were walking along the road, a man said to him, 'I will follow you wherever you go.' Jesus replied, 'Foxes have dens and birds have nests, but the Son of Man has no place to lay his head'" (Luke 9:57-58). In other words, Jesus is asking, "Are you willing to buy into that kind of lifestyle if called?"

"He said to another man, 'Follow me.' But he replied, 'Lord, first let me go and bury my father'" (Luke 9:59). Now, of all the excuses anyone in the world could come up with, that is one of the best. As a local church pastor, I would have excused the man and offered to help him plan the funeral. But not Jesus. "Jesus said to him, 'Let the dead bury their own dead, but you go and proclaim the kingdom of God'" (Luke 9:60). Jesus definitely didn't take a course in pastoral counseling!

I would have thought people would have become kind of quiet at this point, but still another spoke up, "I will follow you, Lord; but first let me go back and say goodbye to my family" (Luke 9:61). Have you ever noticed that so many of us add a "but first" clause onto our commitments? Jesus replies to the man's "but first," "No one who puts a hand to the plow and looks back is fit for service in the kingdom of God" (Luke 9:62). We must ask ourselves, are we following the real Jesus, the Lord of the kingdom of God, or a Jesus of our imaginations? So many of us have baptized our own partisan, political, nationalistic ideas and called them Christian!

Think about the way we describe Santa: "He sees you when you're sleeping. He knows when you're awake. He knows if you've been bad or good!" Our popular notions of Santa Claus reflect the way we have reduced God to a mythical watchdog who judges our niceness or naughtiness and metes out rewards and punishments accordingly.

This is not the God we see in Jesus. Jesus was not the messiah most people were expecting and hoping for. He did not come shimmying down the chimney bearing gifts for good boys and girls.

God's gifts cannot fit in a stocking but must be received in our hearts. Says Simon Tugwell in his book *Prayer*:

> If we keep clamoring for things we want from God, we may often find ourselves disappointed, because we have forgotten the weakness of God and what we may call the poverty of God. We had thought of God as the dispenser of all the good things we would possibly desire; but in a very real sense, God has nothing to give at all except himself.[1]

The picture that you have of God has everything to do with the shaping of your faith and values. If your picture of God is distorted, your life perspective will be skewed. With this faulty image of Jesus as a magical gift giver, it's no wonder our expectations of the Christmas season have become distorted. God doesn't do magic. Magic is an illusion, meant for entertainment rather than transformation. God came to work miracles in our broken world.

The ideal, magical Christmas experience is unattainable. We stress ourselves out and even go into debt to create that warm and fuzzy feeling, both for our families and for ourselves. But that feeling doesn't last. The real meaning of Christmas gets lost in the chaotic clutter of shopping, spending, escalating debt, making exhausting preparations, and building stacks of gifts that most of us don't need or will not ever use. I still find shirts in my closet that I have never worn, given to me who knows how many Christmases ago. In the chaos of the holiday season, we miss the true gift of Immanuel, God with us.

Alan and Deb Hirsch point out in their book *Untamed*:

> Of all the ways culture influences the church, nothing has had more of an impact on us than that of a consumerist vision of society. We have all been impacted by the powerful experience of society that is preoccupied with the acquisition of consumer goods. From good old Santa Claus (a religious symbol co-opted to disciple children in thorough-going materialism from early childhood on) to the complete ubiquity of niche marketing, we are daily being nurtured in the worldview generated by late capitalism of the twenty-first century—*consumerism*.[2]

The idol of consumerism is one of the hardest to topple. John Wesley identified the wallet as the last thing to be converted in a person's life, and Jesus spoke more about money and materialism than any other single topic except the kingdom of God. "No one can serve two masters. Either you will hate the one and love the other, or you will be devoted to the one and despise the other. You cannot serve both God and money" (Matthew 6:24).

Preparing for God's Miracle

Christmas is the celebration of a miracle, but we've edged the miracle worker out of his own birthday. It is time to take it back by planning new traditions that focus on Jesus's presence, rather than the often-forgettable presents we expect to receive.

A *miracle* can be defined as a visible interruption of the laws of nature, understood only by divine intervention and often accompanied by a miracle worker. In other words, a miracle is a unique event in the world that God does through people like you and me. That's right—you are God's miracle worker! You are God's means to effect change in your world. God wants to birth a miracle through you.

You don't feel qualified, you say? You lack the necessary knowledge or have doubts and uncertainties? "Surely there must be someone more worthy and qualified," you protest. Don't sweat it. God doesn't need your *ability*. God will work the miracle through you—all God needs is your *availability* and commitment to act.

Jesus said, "Whoever believes in me, as the Scripture has said, rivers of living water will flow from within them" (John 7:38). Jesus was speaking of the Holy Spirit. The same Holy Spirit that conceived the miracle in Mary's womb indwells every devoted follower of Jesus. In other words, every work of God is conceived in the heart of a disciple, grows in conviction and clarity of vision, and then is delivered through God's intended action, or more simply, God births miracles through ordinary people.

Most of us can relate to being ordinary. From the time we are small children, we become cruelly proficient in developing a social pecking order. Who's cool, smart, and beautiful—and who's not—is often determined in the first weeks of kindergarten, as are the natural leader and the class clown. Where do we find Jesus in the pecking order? In a place of low esteem. He came from a socioeconomic class that was so poor even his own people rejected him. Nazareth was a small village that would not have exposed Jesus to a breadth of educational, cultural, or religious experiences. This is why people questioned the possibility of Jesus's messianic office: "He can't be the Messiah. What good thing could come out of Nazareth?"

While the Scripture gives us no indication of what Jesus looked like, he likely appeared fairly well worn for his relatively young age. In John 8:57, Jesus's opponents remark that he is "not yet fifty years old," suggesting someone who appeared mature beyond his years. While working in refugee camps in Darfur, I was taken aback by the toll that poverty takes on the aging process, often mistaking people in their thirties for being in their fifties. It's unlikely he would have made *People* magazine's list of the fifty most beautiful people or been listed in the high school yearbook as most likely to do anything.

Wow, I can believe in a God who looks like Jesus! I can follow a God who looks like Jesus! And I know that a God who looks like Jesus can use even me!

Throughout Scripture, God chose ordinary, unqualified people through whom to do miracles: the ineloquent Moses, the youngest child David, and the barren Elizabeth. And, of course, Mary. Luke records the words from what has become known as Mary's song:

> *"My soul glorifies the Lord*
> *and my spirit rejoices in God my Savior,*
> *for he has been mindful*
> *of the humble state of his servant."*
> *(Luke 1:46-48)*

The Greek word for *humble* (*tapeinōsis*) means "low or of low degree." Mary came from a very common family, wasn't married, very likely lacked formal education, and did not have the credentials to be a religious leader. What does that say about God's choices and perspective on what it means to be a beautiful and influential person?

Mother Teresa was among the most influential people of our era. Nothing about her physical stature could be considered beautiful or powerful, yet God chose this little Albanian woman to be one of the most powerful representations of Jesus and the resurrection ever seen.

Jesus said, "You will receive power when the Holy Spirit comes on you; and you will be my witnesses" (Acts 1:8). The kind of power that Jesus is talking about is not a power of position, wealth, or prestige. The power of Immanuel is the power to create change in the world through God's action in your life. However, the world is looking for the elaborate, the expensive, and the extraordinary, which is why we miss Jesus. We look for the extraordinary when God uses the ordinary. And the majority of us are ordinary people!

Over the last several years, I have had the privilege of returning to my home high school to do assemblies on leadership and to talk about Ginghamsburg Church's work in Darfur. The students at North College Hill High School in Cincinnati have raised more than $35,000 to build kindergartens in Darfur. What's so amazing about this whole experience is the fact that I am continually invited back to this place where I was once held in very low esteem. I finished the last quarter of my junior year with four Fs and a D–. I was not proficient in academics or athletics. My class ranking was 138 out of 152 (not to mention there were only 144 students by the end of the year, as 8 had dropped out).

Every year, despite my lackluster performance as a juvenile, I am invited back to the same place to speak at assemblies and think, "Yep, there's the corner I sat in for a month" or "There's the desk (and it's the same one from over fifty-five years ago) in the principal's office where I sat before being paddled." Every year, I revisit those places where I was shamed and scorned.

But something happened in 1969: Immanuel—God with me—showed up and awakened in me God's miracle! "'For I know the plans I have for you,' declares the LORD, 'plans to prosper you and not to harm you, plans to give you hope and a future'" (Jeremiah 29:11). In the same way that Jesus once sent his angels to make that announcement to Mary, Jesus comes to ordinary people today to use us for God's purpose. We must only be willing to be used.

Are You Willing to Pay the Price?

Grace may be free, but it is never cheap. Miracles come at a cost. Can you imagine the ostracism and rejection that Mary experienced as an unwed teenager? Becoming pregnant with the Messiah was most definitely not the miracle that she had been hoping for. "Is this what it means to receive God's favor?" she must have wondered. And what about Joseph? Do you think he ever had doubts about the origins of Mary's pregnancy?

At Christmas, we celebrate the birth of the Messiah who was born not only to die sacrificially for us but also to show us how to live sacrificially. *Sacrifice* is not a pleasant word for most of us. Just the idea of it can make us uncomfortable. So it's not surprising that, when all is said and done, most folks would rather have a holly, jolly Christmas than to give themselves as a "womb" for an honest-to-God Christmas miracle.

I received an email several years ago from a person unhappy with the way our Christmas services at Ginghamsburg focused on our work with the Sudan Project. His response really shows how distorted Christians' view of Christmas has become:

> Dear Mr. Slaughter:
>
> Thank you for allowing my family to enjoy the great Christmas services at your church over the last many years. You are a gifted speaker I greatly enjoy listening to. We meet there as a family from all over the area. I am sorry to say that although I understand the great work that needs to be done in Darfur and the work that you have already accomplished, I simply cannot take another African Christmas. I hope this doesn't sound harsh, but our Christmas celebration as a family is not limited to Africa year after year. So this year we will gather in hopes of finding a new worship spot more traditional to the Christmas we know.

How biblical is the "Christmas we know"? Many Christmas traditions that we hold as Christian are really mixtures of traditions: Start with a little biblical truth, blend with some eighteenth-century Victorian practices, and add a double shot of Santa theology (don't hold the whipped cream, please). For example, how many confuse "The Night Before Christmas" with the real Christmas story?

Even our Christmas hymns present a sanitized version of a rather traumatic event: "The cattle are lowing, the poor baby wakes / but little Lord Jesus, no crying he makes." Who can relate to the experience of having a newborn who never cried?

The real Christmas was a snapshot of poverty and anxiety, not feel-good warm fuzzies. But I don't blame that former member for his misunderstanding. We all have grown up with a distorted, acculturated picture of a feel-good Santa Claus Jesus, which has insulated us from God's heart concerning injustice and suffering in the world.

Can't deal with another African Christmas? Think about this: Every five seconds, a child dies somewhere in the world from a hunger-related cause. Let's also not forget that the holy family took flight to Egypt in the face of government-initiated genocide. Jesus spent many formative months in his early childhood as an African refugee. Our tradition tells us that it was a silent night where all was calm and all was bright, but I am not sure that is how Mary and Joseph would have described the experience from their end.

The message of Christmas is about a sacrificial gift. It is easy to feel excited about a newborn warmly wrapped in a manger bed of straw. This Jesus of the cradle poses no threat to our lifestyle and cultural ideologies. But the cradle comes with a cost. You cannot separate the cradle from the cross! The cross is the center of the Christian message. The Apostle Paul put it this way: "I want to know Christ—yes, to know the power of his resurrection and participation in his sufferings" (Philippians 3:10). Jesus, who calls us to follow in the way of the cross, challenges every tradition and value that we hold to be truth. Miracles do not appear out of thin air, like magic. You cannot receive God's miracle unless you are ready and willing to pay the cost.

All of us, to a certain extent, find ways to avoid pain and discomfort. I delay making appointments for my annual checkup because having my blood drawn makes me queasy. We become masters of minimizing risk and maximizing comfort.

Not long ago, I ran into a friend who is about my age and has retired to Florida after a very successful corporate career. He was giving me a hard time about still having to work. I can't imagine not working, since we are put on this earth to be co-creators with God. I retired from the local church in 2017 but then founded Passionate Churches, LLC as a coaching ministry with young pastors. Why has comfortable retirement become the life goal for so many? I asked my friend what he did in all his spare time.

"Oh man, Mike, I get to play golf every day, and my wife and I walk the beach and collect shells."

Is this what the meaning of life comes down to? Endless rounds of golf and shell collections? When we stand before God on the Day of Judgment, will we give an accounting of our golf handicaps and show Jesus our collections? Pardon me, but I passionately desire a more meaningful life purpose.

For our lives to be meaningful, however, we need to give them away. Meaning is not found in personal comfort and material luxuries. So it should be no surprise that a meaningful Christmas is not found in mindless spending, eating, and stressing. Rather, we find meaning when we give sacrificially to those in need, because by doing so, we are giving to Jesus himself. It is his birthday, after all!

I received this email from a young person whom I met when I was speaking at a conference in Kansas City:

> My birthday is December 26, the day after Christmas. I've been a lifelong Christian, and I look forward to the candlelight Christmas Eve service every year. But many times, I think Christmas bleeds into my birthday, and I forget that the gifts I get on December 25 are coming to me for a profoundly different reason than the gifts I get the next day. So that year, for my twentieth birthday, instead of asking for another electronic gadget, I asked my family to help me buy a cow for Heifer International. My mother bought me a child's wooden puzzle in the shape of a cow, and on Christmas morning I opened up each piece individually, with a message written on the back from a family member or friend who had donated money to help me towards my goal. It was one of my best Christmases ever, and I was touched that my family and friends, many of whom are atheists, had helped me bring the world one cow closer to the fulfillment of the kingdom of God.
>
> This year, I plan to take however much money I spend on gifts for others and give a matching amount to Charity: Water, which digs wells to give clean water to people in underdeveloped countries. For the first nineteen years of my life, Christmas and

> my birthday were muddled together, and while I knew in my head that they were not the same thing, I sometimes acted as though December 25 and 26 were Day One and Day Two of my personal gift-getting extravaganza. I now know in my heart that Christmas and my birthday just happen to be right next to each other on the calendar, but that's all they have in common.

Christmas is about a miracle. Miracles don't just happen; they are born through the pains of labor. Pain is not comfortable, and the labor preceding birth is intense, but if we are willing to go through with it, God will conceive miracles in us. Immanuel has come to move us out of our comfort zones.

Said another way, it can be very difficult to make changes in your life that will honor Jesus. But if you are willing to do all that you can, God will do all that you can't. If you're not willing to commit to the pains of labor, however, God won't make the impossible possible.

Conceiving God's Miracle

Every miracle of God is conceived in the heart of a believer, grows in conviction and clarity, and then is delivered through a committed action. As the angel Gabriel said to Mary, "You will conceive and give birth to a son" (Luke 1:31). In other words, you must have a clear picture in your mind of what God wants to accomplish through you before the miracle can become a physical reality. God plants the seeds of miracles in the hearts of available people who are willing to act on God's vision.

Here's an example. Gateway Community (now called Open Table) is a worshiping fellowship made up of people who received food from one of the Ginghamsburg New Path food pantries that serve people throughout the greater Dayton, Ohio area. The people came together every Monday evening for a meal served by different cell groups from the church. The participants worshiped together and were invited to an open table for communion. The seed for the vision of this miracle was planted in the heart of Therese Garison. This is her story in her own words:

> Our cell group had gone once a week to a church downtown to serve the homeless. We would bring in our own cooked food. The place ended up shutting down and our cell group had been praying for God to guide us into our next service area.
>
> Sitting in service one weekend, Mike was doing a series on serving and at one point he asked us to go in silent prayer about something on our hearts, asking for direction, or God's plan, etc. With eyes closed, I asked God, again—with a little attitude this time because I had asked numerous times and I really didn't expect an answer this time either—to lead our group down a clear path of service to others. I clearly heard in my mind and soul, "Why aren't you feeding the people at New Path?" Many clients come hours early for the air conditioning or heat and just sit and wait. I have to admit, I do not remember the rest of the sermon after that because I was questioning whether I was going crazy or not.
>
> I talked about what I'd heard with my husband and later with our cell group. (Pastor Mike always says if you want to know if something is from God to talk it over with other Christian

> brothers and sisters and test it.) It was like a "Duh. Why didn't we think of that before?" moment.
>
> From there, the Holy Spirit took off in all of us and Gateway came alive. My cell group was amazing and helped each week to provide and serve the meal until I was able to get other cell groups, ministry groups, and children's groups to provide complete meals with desserts and drinks.

Now, we not only have a physical meal but a spiritual one as well. A service is provided each week with a meaningful message from Sunday service, including music and communion. This has blessed not only those who are hungry but also those who serve.

We had started in a smaller facility and quickly had to move to our big church to accommodate the crowd. Many now call Gateway their home church. It is the spiritual food, as much as the physical food, that brings them back.

I praise God all the time for knowing exactly when I would be ready to listen, and I am so thankful God let me be a part of God's plan.

Therese was God's agent to carry the message of their mission to her cell group. The vision grew in conviction and clarity in her group, after which the group gave birth to God's miracle. There was no formal institutional church process that needed the approval of committees or administrative boards. Instead, God showed up in the life of an ordinary person and grew the miracle in conjunction with others.

Likewise, God grew the miracle of Jesus through the shepherds who brought Mary encouraging words that she "pondered in her heart," as well as through the angels on the night of Jesus's birth. Later, God also used a devout person named Simeon and the prophet Anna to give clarity to Mary and Joseph's miracle when the couple brought their eight-day-old infant for dedication in the temple. "The child's father and mother marveled at what was said about him" (Luke 2:33). This affirmation would give the new parents focus and fortitude for parenting God's anointed to the fruition of promise.

Every spirit-filled Christian has the potential for a God movement within them. The miracle is conceived and delivered through ordinary people who are willing to dream God's dreams and then act on God's vision. Are you ready for God to birth a Christmas miracle through you?

Questions for Reflection

- How do you picture God? Does this image have more in common with Santa Claus or with Jesus?
- Think about your family's Christmas traditions. How many of them focus on your own comfort and pleasure? What new traditions can you plan that focus more on presence than presents?
- What ideas do you have that could be seeds for a mission miracle? What group are you connected to, or who are some other people that could help make it happen?

Chapter 2

GIVING UP ON PERFECT

Chapter 2

GIVING UP ON PERFECT

The angel said to her, "Do not be afraid, Mary, for you have found favor with God. And now, you will conceive in your womb and bear a son, and you will name him Jesus." Mary said to the angel, "How can this be, since I am a virgin?"

(Luke 1:30-31, 34 NRSV)

National Lampoon's Christmas Vacation, starring Chevy Chase and Beverly D'Angelo, is on my list of top five Christmas movies. It has become a favorite family tradition to watch it with the grandparents and aunts and uncles on Thanksgiving Day. The movie is really a parody about the false expectations that we build up around the traditional family Christmas experience.

Most of us can identify with the character Clark Griswold, who does everything within his control to give his family the gift of a perfect Christmas.

The movie begins with Clark taking his family into the wilderness in search of the perfect Christmas tree. After a road rage accident, which ends with the family station wagon crashing into a snowbank, the Griswolds set off into the wilderness on foot. After a lengthy march in the snow, Clark finds the perfect tree, only to realize that he forgot to bring a saw.

From wrestling with strands of Christmas lights that won't work to suffering with extended visits from abrasive relatives, the Griswolds continue to face experiences that would prompt most of us to say, "Been there, done that."

I can readily identify with the Chevy Chase character. I once had the yuletide experience of assembling my son's Big Wheel at 2 a.m. on Christmas morning, after delivering the midnight candlelight service. (The axle would not fit into the predrilled holes, so I had to drill new ones. Lesson learned—now I pay the assembly fee.) Like Clark, our intentions to plan a "good, old-fashioned family Christmas" fail to live up to the elusive Rockwellian expectations promoted by Madison Avenue marketers.

Consumer-focused marketing and Victorian Christmas traditions have replaced the biblical meaning of "God with us." In our attempts to create the magical Christmas experience, we run ourselves into the ground emotionally, physically, financially, and relationally. Then, after weeks of pressure and preparation, all for the purpose of creating one perfect day in an imperfect year, someone's upset because they didn't get the present they wanted, a toy is already broken, the turkey is burnt, and someone mentioned politics.

The Christmas season, for many, is also a reminder of painful memories. A friend of mine, having just gone through a divorce, said this to me:

> Last year, I was uneasy about Christmas approaching. Since 2002, I had spent most Christmases at my in-laws' place and always enjoyed myself there mightily. Well, my wife moved out last August. Among the scores of other horrible things devouring my mind, there was the thought about Christmas, and for the first time in my life I felt dread toward the holiday.

These words from a Facebook friend echo similar pain:

> The Christmas when my dad left our family was a very sad Christmas. I was about six years old. My aunts and extended family went out of their way to see we still had presents and a Christmas tree. While grateful for the gifts, it was not the presents or the tree that stuck in my mind but [the lesson I learned] years later...that God can and will help you get through the dark times in life.

Christmas may have brought the unexpected to your life this year. But even in the midst of the unexpected, God shows up. Sickness, death, divorce, unemployment. Life gets messy, but in the midst of your mess, God shows up! No matter what you are struggling to overcome, no matter what life issues have come your way, God promises to show up. Christmas is God's vivid reminder that amid the uncertainty, God shows up to bring you peace, purpose, joy, hope, and wholeness.

A Sanitized Nativity

Our Christmas traditions have sanitized the Jesus birth narrative by removing the event from its biblical and historical context. You've seen the Christmas card image countless times: a picturesque, peaceful setting in which "the cattle are lowing" right next to "the little Lord Jesus asleep on the hay." And yet there was nothing clean or neat about the event.

Jesus was born in a stable, a cave where animals were kept. Wherever there are animals, there is dung. And where there is dung, there are flies. I have made multiple trips to Darfur since 2005 to check on Ginghamsburg's projects. Darfur has an arid climate, with temperatures reaching 120-plus degrees Fahrenheit. People make a living by being farmers or herders, so even when we eat, we are never far from sheep, goats, cows, donkeys, chickens, and camels. That means the flies landing on the animal dung are also on our bread, meat, and whatever else we eat. So, clearly, the setting of Jesus's birth was not sanitary. And it didn't get much better from there. Jesus spent his earliest years as a refugee in Egypt, escaping the genocide that Herod was committing in Judea against children aged two and under.

In turn, the Gospel of Luke makes it indelibly clear that walking in the way of Jesus is neither safe nor predictable. Sometimes we have the idea that when we do right, wrong is not supposed to show up, and if we are faithfully following Jesus, then life isn't supposed to get messy. But it does.

In his first chapter, Luke already wants us to understand how complicated the situation is.

In the sixth month [of Mary's cousin Elizabeth's pregnancy], God sent the angel Gabriel to Nazareth, a town in Galilee, to a virgin pledged to be married to a man named Joseph, a descendant of David. The virgin's name was Mary.

(Luke 1:26-27)

By using the word *virgin*, which has a dual meaning of a pubescent girl and one who has not yet had intercourse, Luke is describing this God miracle in the context of an unplanned teenage pregnancy with all of the emotional grief that would entail. How emotionally prepared would a twelve- to fifteen-year-old, Mary's likely age, be for this life experience? How theologically astute would she be to the messianic overtures of the angel's announcement:

Do not be afraid, Mary; you have found favor with God. You will conceive and give birth to a son, and you are to call him Jesus. He will be great and will be called the Son of the Most High. The Lord God will give him the throne of his father David, and he will reign over Jacob's descendants forever; his kingdom will never end.

(Luke 1:30-33)

What part of "do not be afraid" do you think Mary didn't understand? Could it have been the sudden sight of an unexplained celestial event? Did the thought cross her mind that her parents might not believe her explanation, "The Holy Spirit got me pregnant"? We already know that her fiancé, Joseph, rejected her early explanations (Matthew 1:18-19).

It is easy to sanitize the birth event because we approach the story of the Incarnation already knowing the end. It's kind of like missing the experience of a good book or movie because your friend already told you how it turns out. Therefore, we have to understand the Immanuel event in the context of what Mary was experiencing at that moment.

Miracles never happen outside the context of mystery and mess. The miracle of the Incarnation was no exception; however, it begins with the assurance of the angel's promise: "Greetings, you who are highly favored! The Lord is with you" (Luke 1:28). The first premise of faith—knowing that God is with you, that you are favored, and that God is the pursuer in the relationship, regardless of circumstance—begins right here.

There are two Bible verses that my grandmother taught me around the age of four or five that are more profound than anything I learned in twenty-three years of formal education. The first: "For God so loved the world that he gave his one and only Son, that whoever believes in him shall not perish but have eternal life" (John 3:16). The second: "Here I am! I stand at the door and knock. If anyone hears my voice and opens the door, I will come in and eat with that person, and they with me" (Revelation 3:20). By no means do I believe that these verses are in any way exclusive, condemning the billions of non-Christians who ever lived on planet earth to eternal torture. The way of Jesus awakens us to the way of God's love. Accepting Jesus awakens us to our true humanity, our true identity. We are created to love and serve one another.

The message of Christmas is perfectly encapsulated in these two verses—that God not only came to us but also is still here. Our prayers don't invite God's presence. Jesus said, "I'm already here, knocking." Our prayers only recognize the reality that God is here and pursuing a relationship with each of us.

Favored, Not Perfect

God's favor cannot be earned. God comes when we are doing everything wrong. God comes when we are doing nothing. God comes whether we are being naughty or nice. Why?

Because God loves us and we are highly favored! If you are a parent, you understand what it means to favor your children. Without apology, I favor my children over yours. We have all seen the bumper sticker that says something like, "My daughter is a straight-A student at . . . " Of course that parent is proud, but even if your child got straight Ds, you'd still favor them over someone else's A-student every time. It has nothing to do with test scores, behavior, or aptitude. Your children are highly favored by you because they are yours. Likewise, you are highly favored by God because you are God's.

But that does not mean bad things will never happen. Look at the situation from Mary's perspective. She had worked really hard to do what was right, yet it seemed like wrong still showed up. At the moment of the angel's visitation, Mary's limited theological understanding of the messianic promise would not have been at the forefront of her thinking. After all, how theologically astute could this adolescent be? I am pretty sure that, even after he was born, she had no grasp of who Jesus really was, what his ministry would entail, or what kind of pain she would later endure witnessing his suffering and execution. Likely, the only thing on Mary's mind in that moment was, "How will this be . . . since I am a virgin?" (Luke 1:34).

Have you ever found yourself in a similar situation? Maybe you have done everything you know how to be both faithful to God and true to your family, and then you are notified four weeks before the holidays that your job will be discontinued at the end of the year. Or your spouse tells you that they don't love you anymore and wants a divorce. Or your four-year-old is diagnosed with leukemia. Or the high school guidance counselor calls and says they believe your child is using drugs. "How can this be, God, when we have tried so hard to do what is right?"

Now imagine the emotional state of a teenager who just found out she is pregnant and has yet to tell her parents. Not quite sure Mom and Dad bought the "God did it" excuse immediately, if ever, and from that point on, God's blessing would only continue to bring pain into Mary's life—all the way to the foot of her son's cross.

We read the Bible through sanitized lenses because we know the ending at the beginning. But Mary was living in the beginning without the benefit of knowing the Easter morning outcome. How do you think Mary felt after pouring her heart out to the one man who should have supported her but was ready to bail, believing Mary to be a liar? After all, have you ever personally known someone who had a virgin conception? Do you blame Joseph for wanting out?

Can you begin to feel Mary's pain? "What's Mom going to say? My fiancé is seeking legal means against me, and the penalty for adultery is torturous execution. How can this be?"

God's love and favor on us doesn't mean that the path of faith is going to be neat and predictable. I wish it did. By all means, I wish the life of faith would follow a predictable cause-and-effect pattern that always resulted in blessings for the obedient, but it doesn't. Bad things happen to good people.

In the midst of writing this chapter, I received a call from a frantic parent telling me her son was just in a very bad automobile accident and was being flown to an area hospital with multiple broken bones and severe injuries. There have been too many of these emergencies in the over thirty-eight years that my wife, Carolyn, and I have been pastoring Ginghamsburg Church. The most painful are the times that we stand with grieving parents who have just lost a child. I vividly remember one particular Easter Sunday afternoon, after celebrating the miracle of the resurrection with several thousand other believers and seekers. I had barely been home a half hour when the Miami County Sheriff's Department called.

"Mike, can you meet us out at an accident site?" the officer said. "One of the teenagers from your church flipped his car in a cornfield on the way home from your Easter services. We need you to care for his parents while we remove his body from under the car."

"Why, God?" I wondered. "How can this be?"

This wasn't a young man who had been out partying all night. He had been driving home after celebrating the resurrection. Here was a young man who had been doing everything right, and then wrong showed up.

Good people go through the pain of separation and divorce, too. They make sincere promises to each other filled with high hopes and great expectations. They pray, share a common faith, and invest in their children's welfare together. Yet they don't always get what they have asked God to provide. How can that be?

Nowhere does the Bible promise that a life of faith will always make sense or follow a predictable path. Just look at the circumstances surrounding Jesus's birth:

- God sent his son as Savior of the world, yet as a direct consequence of his birth, King Herod murdered untold numbers of babies under the age of two in an attempt to exterminate the "king" that he feared would steal his throne.
- The eleventh chapter of Hebrews, sometimes referred to as the Hall of Faith, celebrates righteous people throughout Scripture. What was the result of their faithfulness? They were tortured and killed.
- The Apostle Paul shares the results of his commitment to live faithfully:

Five times I received from the Jews the forty lashes minus one. Three times I was beaten with rods, once I was pelted with stones, three times I was shipwrecked, I spent a night and a day in the open sea, I have been constantly on the move. I have been in danger from rivers, in danger from bandits, in danger from my fellow Jews, in danger from Gentiles; in danger in the city, in danger in the country, in danger at sea; and in danger from false believers. I have labored and toiled and have often gone without sleep; I have known hunger and thirst and have often gone without food; I have been cold and naked.

(2 Corinthians 11:24-27)

Paul makes it plain to his young protégé, Timothy: "Everyone who wants to live a godly life in Christ Jesus will be persecuted" (2 Timothy 3:12).

Do any of us really understand what we are signing up for when we say yes to Jesus? Reggie McNeal rightly states,

> Church culture in North America is a vestige of the original Christian movement, an institutional expression of religion that is in part a civil religion and in part a club where religious people can hang out with other people whose politics, worldview, and lifestyle match theirs.[1]

The self-focused way that many Western Christian families celebrate Jesus's birth is a painful reminder of just how far the church has strayed from that first-century movement marked by struggle and persecution.

The Gift Amid the Pain

I have often wondered why God entrusted Mary with the responsibility of being the mother of the Savior of the world. She was an immature adolescent who would have probably failed a Bible exam. She would not appear to have the means to provide Jesus with the best resources for a successful future since she came from a very humble background. So why did God choose Mary? Mary had proactive faith. A person with proactive faith doesn't live in the paralysis of doubt and disillusionment. Instead, a person with proactive faith actively pursues God's redemptive purpose and presence in the midst of any situation, even when doing so doesn't make sense.

In response to Mary's question, "How can this be?" the angel told her, "The Holy Spirit will come on you, and the power of the Most High will overshadow you" (Luke 1:35). The Holy Spirit is the presence of God with us and in us, the helper that Jesus promised to send us in his absence: "It is for your good that I am going away. Unless I go away, the Advocate will not come to you; but if I go, I will send him to you" (John 16:7).

Jesus doesn't lie. The Holy Spirit is with you right now to be your helper through any situation, including the messy ones. When life isn't making sense, the power of God will be a shadow over you! That gift, however, is often experienced in pain and suffering. Just remember, God's promise may be delayed, but it will not be denied.

Can I take a moment to share a personal struggle? All my life, I have struggled with doubt. Not the paralyzing, faith-debilitating kind of doubt, but the subtle, nagging, intellectual variety. You and I have been immersed in a modern worldview that has infused our minds with cynicism toward the intervention of the supernatural. In addition, the ideology of postmodern pluralism dances like sugarplums in our heads, making it difficult to accept Jesus's claim as the unique way to truth and life. Many times I have wished that Jesus would appear and give me just one visible sign of his presence, or maybe even an audible voice.

Do you struggle with these kinds of doubts? I know I'm not alone in this. The angel who showed up to let Mary know she was pregnant just disappeared, leaving God's favored one standing in silence. No more directions, no signed note from God to give to her mother—just silence!

Mother Teresa's decades-long battle with feeling God's absence also gives me hope. She spoke of the "darkness of faith," referring to the almost-four-decade period of her ministry during which she felt an absence of God's presence. "Jesus has a very special love for you," she told the Reverend Michael Van Der Peet in September 1979. "As for me, the silence and the emptiness is so great that I look and do not see, listen and do not hear."[2]

The human struggle with doubt goes all the way back to the first biblical account of man and woman. Evil's strategy was to plant the seed of distrust in Eve's worldview about God's loving goodness. However, the account given in the Genesis story reminds us that God is never the one who is hiding (see Genesis 3:8-10). We hide behind the elusive covers of doubt, fear, guilt, anger, indifference, misguided religious traditions, and self-focus. But God is always there with us, even in the midst of our struggles.

God came to earth as a baby who was thrust into the experience of the oppressed refugees of the world. God came as the victim, not the victor, fully identifying with the marginalized—the child sold into slavery, the Jew in a concentration camp, the child infected with HIV, and the orphan in Darfur. Christmas is the story of this vulnerable God-turned-human, who became a refugee in Africa. And God continues to show up in such places of pain.

There is a picture hanging on the wall of my office of a little girl in a remote village in South Darfur. My son took this picture in 2007 when we were there checking up on a water system that had been constructed through Ginghamsburg's partnership with the United Methodist Committee on Relief (UMCOR).

The young girl is using an empty USAID food bag as a cloak in the picture. I had never heard of USAID in 2007, but through research found out that literally thousands of children like her depended on USAID for survival. One of the first acts of the second Trump administration was to eliminate USAID without realizing the impact on children like this. Estimates on the internet range from 330,00 to 760,000 deaths since USAID has been dismantled. Lord God, have mercy!

A Little Help from Your Friends

God never intended for you to handle life's unexpected turns by yourself. The life of faith is developed and encouraged within the context of community. Before the angel Gabriel left Mary, he named a mentor for her—Mary's cousin Elizabeth. "Even Elizabeth your relative is going to have a child in her old age, and she who was said to be unable to conceive is in her sixth month" (Luke 1:36). God was leading Mary to someone who had already experienced some of what Mary was going through. In turn, Elizabeth's experience would become the fertilizer of hope and encouragement for Mary's miracle. The wisdom of Elizabeth's years had provided her with a wise, well-traveled faith perspective, which she drew upon to help lead Mary.

Likewise, God shows up and speaks to us through others who have experienced similar struggles and come out on the other side. That means your experiences of pain and, eventually, hope can also become the seed for God's miracle in someone else's life.

Recovery communities refer to these people as *sponsors.* They act as mentor guides who have successfully been through a recovery program and have worked the Twelve Steps. A mentor is a more experienced leader who helps a less experienced protégé, just as Paul mentored Timothy: "And the things you have heard me say in the presence of many witnesses entrust to reliable people who will also be qualified to teach others" (2 Timothy 2:2). Who was a contagious follower of Jesus who mentored you?

Carolyn and I have been very open with others about the problems that we have experienced in our marriage, including a period about thirty-five years ago when we were considering divorce, until God showed up in a way that can be described as nothing short of miraculous. The healing we experienced as a result was not without pain and even today involves much hard work. But we love each other deeply, and divorce will never again be an option. Carolyn is my best friend, and our relationship has become a priority to me over our church and ministry. (For those of you not in professional ministry, I must explain that pastors can have a tendency to place their ministries above their families and use God as the excuse. This may explain the root problems in the first half of our marriage.)

Carolyn is often asked by pastors and their spouses to travel with me to conferences to speak about the struggles that we have had in our marriage. This is how that conversation usually goes:

Pastor: "Tell us, Carolyn, about how Mike was a donkey's behind and why he is not one now."

Carolyn: "No, no. He's still a donkey's behind, but now he's a loving donkey's behind."

Why are we asked to travel great distances to share our struggles? Because our painful experiences become seeds of hope for God's miracle in someone else's life. Isn't it amazing how God works?

John Wagner is a committed follower of Jesus who used his gifts and talents to serve in Ginghamsburg Church's music ministry. He was also a popular singer in local area clubs. His wife, Rexann, was a public school superintendent in an at-risk school district and had chaired our church board in the past. John was diagnosed with multiple sclerosis (MS) several years ago, and the disease has progressed very aggressively. John inspired me as I watched him struggle up on the platform to lead the congregation in singing songs of praise and thanksgiving to God. It took incredible effort for him to get up and back down with some help from friends. Here is John's story in his own words:

> When I was diagnosed with MS in May 2006 I had no idea the journey God had in store for me. While MS symptoms were present—my handwriting was shaky, my legs tingling, and my coordination somewhat impaired—life was pretty much marching along as usual. I was a hard-working warehouseman with twenty-seven-plus years at the same company, a vivacious, in-demand entertainer, and a child of the Lord. I had two wonderful daughters and a classy, loving wife. Life was good.
>
> My progressive type of MS soon began its relentless rampage of my body and no longer allowed me to work. Walking on my own accord soon progressed to walking with a cane, then walking with a walker, and now using a mobility scooter. Medication side effects impact my daily life causing dizziness, nausea, inability to move my legs, and general fatigue and malaise. And, in all this, all I can think about is how thankful I

> am. So thankful to God that I still have my limbs, that He has allowed me to sing his praise with the church music ministry, that He slowed me down to appreciate the subtle blessings I so often ignored. The birds singing in the mornings, the beauty of the butterflies, the laughter of children—I now marvel and praise Him for these. He has so blessed me by removing a sense of arrogance and "me-focus" that was present before, and has replaced it with thankfulness and humbleness. My children, my wife, my friends, and even total strangers take such good care of me. Having MS has opened my spirit to the beauty of others' spirits and I have never doubted that His purpose in this will continue to be revealed. Yes, I have MS, but MS doesn't have me. And life is still good because God is good—all the time.

John's continued commitment to keep showing up to serve and his relentless attitude of gratitude never failed to lift me up. Life doesn't always make sense; life gets messy even for the faithful. But God uses our painful experiences to become the seeds of hope for others' miracles.

Why did God choose Mary to be the mother of Jesus? Because God knew that even when life didn't make sense, she would choose to continue to serve God. "I am the Lord's servant. . . . May your word to me be fulfilled" (Luke 1:38). Mary didn't quit through the years of Jesus's upbringing. Mary didn't quit when the religious authorities accused her son of blasphemy. She didn't quit while standing at the foot of her son's cross, when life undoubtedly seemed insane. Mary taught Jesus that we serve God even when life doesn't make sense.

After all, life isn't about you and me. We miss life when we use God to get what we desire instead of allowing ourselves to be used by God for God's desires. When we default to our own self-centered expectations, we take a faith detour on our life journey.

So when Christmas comes around during an imperfect season of life, and you just don't feel like celebrating, remember: It's not your birthday; it's Jesus's birthday, and by celebrating Christmas, we are celebrating someone else who suffered, too.

Life is not about staying safe and living comfortably. The call to follow Jesus is a call to give your life to him, to join God's mission in healing the souls of the world. We were never promised a reward in this life. The real rewards are found in the joy and peace that we experience through serving others in Christ's spirit. This is why we can pray, "I am your servant, Lord. Regardless of what comes my way, let it be done to me according to your will, even when the angels disappear."

Even in the midst of the unexpected, the messy, and the devastating, you can still fully expect God to show up. No matter what you are struggling to overcome, God promises to show up. This is truly what Christmas is about: In the midst of all our messes—poverty, genocide, environmental disasters, wars, terrorism, religious hate and bigotry, divorce, cancer, and, yes, even death—God shows up!

Questions for Reflection

- What is your vision of a perfect Christmas? What imperfect circumstances will you face this year that will challenge your ability to celebrate Christmas fully?
- How do you think Mary felt in the months and days leading up to Jesus's birth? How does her experience of the first Christmas influence the way you approach the holiday season?
- How can you celebrate Jesus in the midst of your struggles? How can God use your struggles to help others this Christmas?

Chapter 3

SCANDALOUS LOVE

Chapter 3

SCANDALOUS LOVE

Then the LORD said to me, "Go and love your wife again, even though she commits adultery with another lover. This will illustrate that the LORD still loves Israel, even though the people have turned to other gods and love to worship them."

(Hosea 3:1 NLT)

Christmas is the anticipated time of year when family members gather from different corners of the country and beyond to celebrate the best of what we hold dear in our relationships. Yet, for some, it can also represent the ominous presence of past hurts and even current relationship pain, making Christmas depressing or lonely.

Carolyn and I see Christmas as a great opportunity to celebrate the gift of family. Before we retired in 2017, we couldn't go away because of our responsibilities at church, so everyone came to our place. We were fortunate at the time to have parents (all of whom have since passed) who were able to celebrate with us, along with our children and grandchildren and their uncles and aunts. We have had as many as sixteen people stay in our home for three days straight, with children sleeping on couches, an aunt and uncle on a pullout in the basement, and Carolyn and me on a blow-up mattress in the den.

Part of our family tradition—to see a movie together the day after Christmas—has been modified a bit since we have become grandparents. Now Papa and Nana (that's us) stay at home with the grandkids, while our children have a date night at the movies. Last year, after putting our granddaughter to bed, Carolyn and I watched the movie *He's Just Not That Into You* on DVD. The movie is about a young single woman named Gigi who is caught up in a cycle of superficial serial dating. Gigi repeatedly misreads comments and actions from her male dates as authentic interest. After each date, which tends to culminate in a brief bedroom encounter, Gigi returns home and obsessively sits by the phone, waiting for the call that never comes.

Everyone wants to know that they are important to someone. Remember how kids passed notes back and forth in grade school: "I like you. Do you like me? Check yes, no, or maybe." That's because God created us for intimate, authentic relationships.

Unfortunately, we are all capable of compromising our most fundamental beliefs to make such intimate connections. Why else do people stay in abusive relationships or commit to others who have conflicting belief structures?

Some of us are late bloomers. When I graduated from high school, I was five feet eleven and weighed something like 120 pounds. There was nobody special knocking at my door. Have you ever experienced rejection? All of us will at some point in our lives.

Is it any wonder that we learn early on to portray ourselves as being someone other than who we really are and create layers of emotional defenses to protect ourselves from relational pain?

Worse, our esteem deficiencies carry over into our relationship with God. Most of us have no problem believing in God but struggle with being secure in God's belief in us. Do you ever think, "How can God believe in me? How could God ever possibly desire me?" Most of us become pretty adept at hiding our imperfections and deficiencies from others while being fully aware that we can't hide them from God.

But what do we do in response? Just like Adam and Eve, we run and hide from the sound of God's approaching footsteps because of our very real sense of shame. You and I are the ones who have created this emotional barrier. We are the ones running away. God is neither emotionally detached nor hiding from us.

Christmas is the heralding of God who comes to be with us. God is the one who pursues. The Incarnation is the revelation of God's scandalous love affair with humanity!

One of the most passionate illustrations of God's love affair with humanity is found in the book of Hosea. During Israel's last days of growth and prosperity under Jeroboam II (2 Kings 14:23-29), the Israelites became lukewarm in their faith and strayed, as God's people often do in prosperous times.

Once again, Israel had wandered from the Lord, who had brought them out of slavery and made them God's own unique covenant people.

From a human perspective, we can equate God's relationship with the Israelites to the sacred trust commitment made and then broken in marriage. That is why Hosea denounced Israel's behavior as the worst kind of infidelity (Hosea 1:2). Later, Jesus made a similar reference when speaking about the struggle between materialism and our faith focus, by saying, "No one can serve two masters. Either you will hate the one and love the other, or you will be devoted to the one and despise the other" (Matthew 6:24).

God demonstrates unrelenting love for God's people through Hosea by telling him to go and marry a "promiscuous woman and have children with her, for like an adulterous wife this land is guilty of unfaithfulness to the LORD" (Hosea 1:2). The suggestion is bold and outrageous. Can you imagine marrying someone you knew would be unfaithful? Who would ever knowingly set themselves up for such a life of hell?

To fully understand this biblical analogy, we must go back to God's unique commitment to his covenant people, Israel. Of all the peoples on the earth with whom God could forge a covenant-binding relationship, God chose a rather obscure people, and one of the smallest, most picked-on tribes to ever exist on the planet. Why? Beauty is in the eye of the beholder, and love cannot be defined rationally. We do know, however, that God certainly didn't choose Israel on the basis of merit or moral fortitude. (After all, no human being can claim either, according to Romans 3:23.) In addition, God willfully entered into this "marriage" knowing full well that God's people would be unfaithful.

Hosea represents God's relentless pursuing love, and Hosea's unfaithful wife, Gomer, represents God's people—not only the Israelites but also you and me.

Our Infidelity

We have been created to find life and meaning through exclusive devotion to our lover, God, but in the spirit of prostitution, we sell ourselves out to materialism and greed. This is never more obvious than in the way we celebrate Jesus's birth: in a self-focused, hedonistic feast of gluttony, oblivious to what God really wants from us. Imagine Gomer saying, "Happy Birthday, Hosea! To celebrate, I'm going to party with my other friends!" What God wants from us, for Jesus's birthday and every day, is love. God craves for us to return God's scandalous love with our own, demonstrated by how we treat those in need.

God is not oblivious to the fact that one child dies every five seconds of a hunger-related cause and that as many as seven will have died by the time you have finished reading this page.[1] God also knows that one child dies every two minutes from malaria, which could be prevented by a simple mosquito net that costs less than $10.[2] It is not a secret to God that each year in Darfur, as many as sixty thousand children die from dehydration due to diarrhea caused by water-borne illnesses.[3] Jesus also made his feelings on such matters crystal clear: "Truly I tell you, whatever you did for one of the least of these brothers and sisters of mine, you did for me" and "whatever you did not do for one of the least of these, you did not do for me" (Matthew 25:40, 45).

Hosea's desanitized version of God's scandalous love is really what the meaning of the Incarnation is all about. Gomer's adultery represents the idolatry of God's covenant people. As baptized followers of Jesus, we are children of that covenant which calls us back from our adultery, whether we made that vow of commitment or our parents made it for us. Some of us can't remember our baptisms because our parents brought us before the community of faith for this sacrament when we were infants. Our parents marked us and gave us to God for God's exclusive purpose. In other words, whether we like it or not, God holds us accountable for our parents' promise—we're stuck!

The Hosea message vividly illustrates the crux of the Christmas Incarnation. God tells Hosea, "Go, show your love to your wife again, though she is loved by another man and is an adulteress. Love her as the LORD loves the Israelites" (3:1).

Now put yourself emotionally for a moment in Hosea's shoes. Your spouse is living with another man, has committed multiple adulteries, shows no interest in you, and has never even asked you to come and bail her out of her self-imposed slavery. Who in their right mind would go rescue her and then bring her back to their own bed?

Make her the mother of your children again? No way! Love her as God loves Israel? Are you kidding?

Yet this scandalous biblical account testifies to the outrageous, pursuing love of God for a broken world. This is the desanitized version of the Christmas story: God loves us and wants us even while we remain under the influence of unworthy lovers such as greed, selfishness, addiction, and deceit. So God has come to buy us back! The magnitude of this kind of love is beyond my comprehension, but after all, beauty is in the eye of the beholder.

Trusting the Promise

Mary had every reason to feel betrayed and abandoned by God. She was a young teen, unmarried, and pregnant. Imagine all the layers of economic and social complexity that such an incident would carry for a female adolescent in first-century Judea. We can't remove Mary from the sometimes-difficult realities of the culture. And don't forget the possible legal ramifications: death by stoning.

Luke implies that Mary knew the humiliation that comes from poverty. The Greek word used in Mary's song to describe her life situation is *tapeinous* (Luke 1:52), which means low in situation, humble, poor. I get a much better perspective on Mary's life situation by observing the severe consequences of poverty on the women and children in Darfur, where they spend up to eight hours a day traveling back and forth just to get water. These people experience the humiliation not only of poverty but also of war, rape, and genocide, which might not be too dissimilar to Mary's experience of living under a repressive Roman regime.

Through all this confusion, Mary clung to the promise of God, holding tightly to the angel's words: "Greetings, you who are highly favored! The Lord is with you" (Luke 1:28). And despite Mary's confused and emotionally troubled reaction in verse 29, from the depths of her being we also hear the harmonious sounds of hope and faith:

> *"My soul glorifies the Lord*
> *and my spirit rejoices in God my Savior,*
> *for he has been mindful*
> *of the humble state of his servant.*
> *From now on all generations will call me blessed,*
> *for the Mighty One has done great things for me—*
> *holy is his name."*
>
> *(Luke 1:46-49)*

It didn't matter what anyone else in the community would think or say about her condition. Mary hung onto the promise of God and responded with a song of daring, boundless faith. Her focus was not on her emotional state or on her challenging situation but on the scandalous love of God, who promised her a future of hope: "My soul glorifies the Lord!"

The Christmas story exemplifies how God's ways are not our ways. We may dismiss people of such low esteem as Mary, people whose lives are marred by humiliation and scandal, but God works miracles in unexpected places, in unexpected ways. Mary trusted in God's promise, knowing God's scandalous way of working good out of seemingly bad situations.

Do you trust God's promise to redeem your life? To love you and want your love in return, no matter what kind of mess your life has been? This is the scandalous love we testify to when we profess faith in Jesus Christ. You may be saying one thing with your lips but quite another from your spiritual core. Mary's core magnified the Lord. That means that in the company of others, her presence and attitude made God more visible. Is your presence making God more visible in the lives of the people with whom you come into contact on a daily basis?

You might find yourself at this moment in a challenging and frustrating life season. I am writing this chapter during the war between Iran and the United States and its impact on rapidly rising gas prices and the effect on global economies, not to mention the loss of innocent lives. The effects of up-and-down economic growth in recent years and rising consumer debt have stripped away savings and deferred dreams. Children's college funds have been eroded and 401(k)s depleted. Many have been forced into unemployment and early retirement. Others have taken dramatically reduced incomes. You may be among the growing number of Americans aged fifty-five and older who have put their retirement dreams on hold and now face a dismal financial future. The rate of home foreclosures continued to rise in the fall of 2024, while most Americans found themselves struggling under the weight of debt.

Or your challenge could be closer to home: a life-threatening illness, the death of a loved one, the severe consequences of addiction, or the pain of divorce—all have the potential to be utterly devastating.

Regardless, it can be easy in difficult times to get derailed and lose your God-bearings.

Some of you reading this haven't been listening to the angel's promise that, like Mary, you are a favored child of God—that God is with you. Rather, you have been listening to the lord of lies who tells you, "You have royally screwed up. You have disappointed God. You are not favored, and God will never be with you." Don't listen to these lies. Listen to the promises of God.

The Bible contains the testimonials of innumerable failures who went from zeros to heroes as they learned to live by faith, embracing God's grace. David, despite his courageous faith (check out his exploits against the Philistine champion Goliath and others in 1 and 2 Samuel and 1 and 2 Kings), committed adultery with Bathsheba and had her husband murdered. What a royal disaster!

Grace, God's scandalous love, is what the message of Christmas is all about. Despite our failures, God wants us and comes to redeem us. Despite his failure, David chose to sing of God's promise:

> *For you created my inmost being;*
> *you knit me together in my mother's womb.*
> *I praise you because I am fearfully and wonderfully made;*
> *your works are wonderful,*
> *I know that full well.*
> *My frame was not hidden from you*
> *when I was made in the secret place,*
> *when I was woven together in the depths of the earth.*
> *Your eyes saw my unformed body;*
> *all the days ordained for me were written in your book*
> *before one of them came to be.*
>
> *How precious to me are your thoughts, God!*
> *How vast is the sum of them!*
>
> *(Psalm 139:13-17)*

Those who have messed up most respond with the greatest gratitude for God's relentless love.

In the third chapter of Revelation, Jesus chastises the church in Laodicea.

> *I know your deeds, that you are neither cold nor hot. I wish you were either one or the other! So, because you are lukewarm—neither hot nor cold—I am about to spit you out of my mouth. You say, "I am rich; I have acquired wealth and do not need a thing." But you do not realize that you are wretched, pitiful, poor, blind and naked.*
>
> *(Revelation 3:15-17)*

The Laodiceans professed Christ, but they placed their trust in monetary success and sought meaning in the accumulation of material possessions. Like so many church folk, the Laodiceans believed in God but lived their daily lives as though they didn't need God. They were self-reliant, taking the controls and navigating most of life's challenges while giving God no more than a casual nod. What an accurate description of the twenty-first-century church in America. We are so wealthy that we do not realize our desperate need for God. Is it any wonder the majority of Americans don't take the Gospel seriously and that the eighteen-to-thirty-five-year-old generation sees the church in such a negative light?

Practicing Scandalous Love

The worst kind of fool is the person who believes that God exists but lives life without taking God's directives seriously. It is way too easy to honor God with our mouths while we worship at the altar of our own desires. We've put ourselves in the place of God, but Jesus reminds us that we can have only one true life devotion. Jesus was very clear. We can't serve two masters (Matthew 6:24)!

Only when we realize how far we have strayed from the one who loves us so deeply and unconditionally can we respond in radical faith. And when we passionately pursue God as our defining life center, then everything else will be rightly ordered.

There is going to be a role reversal when Jesus comes back. The Bible says that God opposes the proud but gives grace to the humble. The humble know that they are handicapped. The humble know they need the mercy of God because they don't deserve God's mercy. But when Jesus returns, those who have been despised and insulted will be exalted, and those who have been rich and self-consumed will end up poor. We can practice God's kind of scandalous love when we see people through the lens of this reversal. Rather than praising the rich, we will lift up the poor. Rather than condemning those facing trials, we will support them and offer encouragement.

When Mary faced the shocking and confusing news of her virgin pregnancy, she immediately sought out wise, godly counsel from her older cousin Elizabeth. There is no question that this young pregnant teen would be hit with plenty of criticism and ostracism by her community. Mary didn't need negativity; she needed encouragement and accountability from a godly source. The first words that this confused young girl heard from her cousin's mouth were an encouraging reminder: "Blessed are you among women, and blessed is the child you will bear!" (Luke 1:42). The word *bless* means "to speak well or approvingly of." Mary would experience enough backbiting and condemnation from everyone else. She would receive a magnitude of discouraging words, but thankfully, Elizabeth saw the promise in her cousin's situation.

How many miracles are aborted because of put-downs, sarcasm, and negativity? We cannot carry God's miracles full-term apart from the encouragement, fellowship, and accountability that comes from being connected to a tight network of mature sisters and brothers of faith who encourage us in God's purpose. Let us be promise bearers for one another. Let us remind people of God's miraculous, scandalous way of reversing the tide, as Elizabeth did when she said, essentially, "Don't quit, Mary. In time, people will honor God's name because of you. They may be demeaning your character now, but someday your name will be held in high esteem."

Carolyn and I lead a discipleship group in our home. Thirty-one people in their twenties and thirties packed into our family room for the purpose of study, accountability, and encouragement. At one such meeting, a single mom shared with us how understanding the scandal of Mary's pregnancy and Jesus's birth gave her hope to trust in God's love and help others do the same:

> I was raised in a Christian home, but when I became a teenager I went through a stage of rebellion that led me into becoming pregnant. Hearing Mike's Christmas message, which went into details of the adversity that Mary faced, is what pulled me through. Mary, pregnant as a young teen, was able to hold steadfast in the face of ridicule and uncertainty. She fully trusted God's will for her and submitted herself to him. The message was encouragement to help me become more serious with my walk with Jesus. I went on to graduate high school and marry the father of the child and have another son, but due to infidelity, our marriage ended in divorce. Finding myself single

> with two kids and living on a limited income has been hard, but acquiring a thankful heart and buying almost everything used, we are able to make it. God has now put this passion for pregnant teens in my heart, which has led me to get involved with an organization that helps pregnant teens and young women. I am now able to encourage young teens to practice chastity before marriage and pregnant teens to choose life and finish high school. This has become proof to me that God takes all things and uses them to benefit others. He equips us with what we need to help even if it is just a set of listening ears, a story to share, and a heart to serve.

Broken people more easily recognize their need for a Savior. When we are connected to others, it is much easier to truly understand and trust God's power and promise to transform our circumstances, and we can't help responding with a passionate, radical love of our own.

In the book of Hosea, we never find out whether Gomer gave up her infidelity for good and lived with Hosea as a loving wife. The last we hear, Hosea bought her back for fifteen shekels, some barley, and some wine. He told his wife that she had to stay with him for a certain number of days, to symbolize Israel's time in exile (Hosea 3:1-4). Hosea had no way of knowing whether his wife would love him in return, but his prophecy in the very next verse (v. 5) indicates that there was some hope: "Afterward the Israelites will return and seek the LORD their God and David their king. They will come trembling to the LORD and to his blessings in the last days."

When forgiveness is offered, wandering people are drawn back home. Though we may not deserve it, God showed us mercy and sent God's son to show us the way home. Jesus came to earth as a tiny baby in humble, scandalous circumstances to redeem and restore broken places and broken hearts. That is the love we celebrate at Christmas, and it is that kind of love that we are called to show in return.

Questions for Reflection

- Do you really believe that God loves you madly, passionately, unconditionally? Think about the deepest, most enduring relationships you've experienced—with a parent, a spouse, a friend, or a child. If these are but a glimpse of the relationship God wants with you, what must that mean about God's love?
- God promises to bring good out of bad, to raise up the lowly, and to comfort the afflicted. How would you view your life if you trusted completely in those promises?
- What would it mean for us to love others "scandalously"? How would that be different from the safe, cautious ways we often show Christ's love in the world?

Chapter 4

JESUS'S WISH LIST

Chapter 4

JESUS'S WISH LIST

"The King will reply, 'Truly I tell you, whatever you did for one of the least of these brothers and sisters of mine, you did for me.'"
(Matthew 25:40)

Every Christmas, I go through the challenging routine of selecting the perfect gift for my wife, Carolyn. We remind ourselves that it's Jesus's birthday, not our own, and that we are not supposed to spend too much on each other. The ground rules we establish make the quest for a meaningful gift somewhat difficult, but one particular Christmas, I hit the royal jackpot.

Our daughter and then-son-in-law, who lived in Boston at the time, were planning to vacation in Orlando with our then-ten-month-old granddaughter (who is now seventeen at this writing) just five weeks after Christmas. Our daughter called me and invited us to spend their vacation with them. What a great opportunity to babysit our granddaughter so that her mommy and daddy could grab some much-needed time alone! I immediately booked two tickets using my frequent-flier miles, wrapped the itinerary, and placed it under the tree.

You should have seen Carolyn's face on Christmas morning when she opened the box. The cost was minimal; the experience priceless. The only problem now is that I've never figured out how to top that gift in the years that have followed.

Do you struggle to come up with the perfect gifts each Christmas for the special people in your life? It can be tough, but here's an even more important question: What do you give Jesus on his birthday? This question brings us back to the real focus of this book: Christmas is not your birthday! It is Jesus's birthday.

How can we change the traditional focus of Christmas from materialistic self-indulgence to giving Jesus what he desires on his birthday? How can we make it less about us and more about him? And what can you possibly give the Lord of the universe? Fortunately, Jesus made his wish list unquestionably clear. The book of Matthew contains Jesus's related discourse, concerning his return and the day of final judgment:

> *"When the Son of Man comes in his glory, and all the angels with him, he will sit on his glorious throne. All the nations will be gathered before him, and he will separate the people one from another as a shepherd separates the sheep from the goats. He will put the sheep on his right and the goats on his left.*

> *"Then the King will say to those on his right, 'Come, you who are blessed by my Father; take your inheritance, the kingdom prepared for you since the creation of the world. For I was hungry and you gave me something to eat, I was thirsty and you gave me something to drink, I was a stranger and you invited me in, I needed clothes and you clothed me, I was sick and you looked after me, I was in prison and you came to visit me.'"*
>
> *(Matthew 25:31-36)*

When Jesus spoke these words to his disciples, they were absolutely befuddled. For two years, they had been with Jesus virtually 24/7 and had never seen Jesus in any of these predicaments. But then Jesus continued, clarifying his meaning: "The King will reply, 'Truly I tell you, whatever you did for one of the least of these brothers and sisters of mine, you did for me'" (v. 40). Jesus made the meaning of discipleship perfectly clear: you can't separate your relationship with God from your responsibility for God's people.

The Epistle of 1 John says our direct involvement in meeting people's physical needs is primary evidence of our rebirth in Christ. "We know that we have passed from death to life, because we love each other. Anyone who does not love remains in death" (1 John 3:14). The evangelist goes on to define love in a very concrete way:

> *This is how we know what love is: Jesus Christ laid down his life for us. And we ought to lay down our lives for our brothers and sisters. If anyone has material possessions and sees a brother or sister in need but has no pity on him, how can the love of God be in that person? Dear children, let us not love with words or speech but with actions and in truth.*
>
> *(1 John 3:16-18)*

We serve God when we serve others. We give to Jesus when we sacrifice our time, talents, and resources to meet others' needs in his name. The church is the body of Christ. We are the only hands, feet, and wallets that God has!

YOU Give Them Something to Eat

Even during his earthly ministry, Jesus wanted his followers to know that they were responsible for feeding the hungry in their midst. Consider the famous feeding of the five thousand. Jesus had just heard about the gruesome death of his cousin, John the Baptizer. John had been openly censuring Herod for taking his sister-in-law as his own wife. Herod was afraid of the potential negative political blowback generated by John's unrelenting preaching. John's prophetic confrontation with Herod literally cost John his head.

You can imagine the emotional impact this news had on Jesus. The Gospel of Matthew gives the most detailed account, reporting that Jesus sought solitude in a remote place to deal with his grief. But the crowds just wouldn't leave him alone. People from all of the surrounding towns sought him out, and we aren't talking about a typical Sunday-morning-church kind of crowd. We are talking about five thousand men, along with women and children, which may equate to more than twenty thousand people. Needless to say, this created a logistics problem equivalent to that of the modern-day rock festival. Concessions, food, and beverage service—if only the disciples had had some forewarning, they could have planned. Instead, they ran to Jesus with the next-best strategy: "Send the crowds away, so they can go to the villages and buy themselves some food" (Matthew 14:15). What Jesus says next gives us the clearest insight into God's economy: "They do not need to go away. You give them something to eat" (v. 16).

The resources of heaven do not fall from the sky; they are released through God's people! God creates miracles through the resources that you and I hold in our hands. Moses' staff, David's five smooth stones, the widow's oil, six water jars at a wedding reception, another widow's two small coins, and a boy's lunch comprising five pieces of bread and two small fish—these are the resources that miracles are made of!

"But we only have five loaves of bread and two fish," the disciples answered.

"But we are living in a time of rising prices and economic uncertainty," we might say today.

"But you don't understand, Jesus; we can't afford to pay both the mortgage and a health care premium in the same month."

"But Jesus, we are just a small struggling church and don't have the resources." When Carolyn and I came to Ginghamsburg Church in 1979, it was a small two-room country church built in 1876, with a yearly budget of $27,000, in a community of twenty-two houses. "But pastor, you don't understand. You come from the big city (Cincinnati). We are just simple country folk who can barely afford to keep the lights on."

"But . . . but . . . but . . ." It is time to commit to losing our big "buts"! After all, Jesus doesn't save us to get us into heaven but to get heaven into us. Jesus saves us for the purpose of channeling the resources of heaven onto earth. Jesus needs the five loaves and two fish that you have in your hand, no matter how futile your financial situation may seem.

> *"Bring them here to me," he said. And he directed the people to sit down on the grass. Taking the five loaves and the two fish and looking up to heaven, he gave thanks and broke the loaves. Then he gave them to the disciples, and the disciples gave them to the people.*
> *(Matthew 14:18-19)*

It is important for us to note the sequence of events. Jesus takes the five loaves and two fish from the disciples, blesses them, and then gives them back to the disciples to distribute. The resources that God uses to multiply miracles to meet people's needs come from our hands. When we obediently release what is in our hands, Jesus blesses it, multiplies it, and then gives it back to us for the purpose of distribution. This is Kingdom Economics 101. We must release what is in our hands to increase for God's purpose! I mentioned that when I came to Ginghamsburg in 1979, the yearly budget was $27,000. When we left in 2017, the yearly budget was $5.4 million, not counting the $8 million we raised for our projects in Darfur, $1 million for Imagine No Malaria, and several million for other humanitarian projects. It is absolutely amazing what God can do in a small country church with a $27,000 annual budget when we are willing to release for God's increase!

Our willingness to obey Jesus's directive to release what is in our hands can literally mean life or death for hundreds of thousands of people around the world. I have already mentioned, as an example, that one child dies every two minutes from a malaria-related cause that can be prevented by a simple mosquito net at a cost of less than $10.

Also consider 2 Corinthians 9:6-9:

> *Remember this: Whoever sows sparingly will also reap sparingly, and whoever sows generously will also reap generously. Each of you should give what you have decided in your heart to give, not reluctantly or under compulsion, for God loves a cheerful giver. And God is able to bless you abundantly, so that in all things at all times, having all that you need, you will abound in every good work. As it is written:*
>
> *"They have freely scattered their gifts to the poor;*
> *their righteousness endures forever."*

Notice the priority placed on our responsibility for the poor in God's economy. Verses 10 and 11 go on to say this:

> *Now he who supplies seed to the sower and bread for food will also supply and increase your store of seed and will enlarge the harvest of your righteousness. You will be enriched in every way so that you can be generous on every occasion, and through us your generosity will result in thanksgiving to God.*

God releases the resources of heaven through obedient people. You are created to be the channel through which God's blessings flow to meet the needs of God's children. But Jesus needs what you are holding in your hand. With the rising cost of food prices, it might be as simple as picking up a few extra items at the grocery store for your local food pantry. Listen closely to the Spirit. The Spirit will guide you!

Good News for the Poor

Jesus began his public ministry in his hometown of Nazareth by boldly declaring his mission statement, which he read from the text of Isaiah 61:

> *The Spirit of the Sovereign* LORD *is on me,*
> *because the* LORD *has anointed me*
> *to proclaim good news to the poor.*
> *He has sent me to bind up the brokenhearted,*
> *to proclaim freedom for the captives*
> *and release from darkness for the prisoners,*
> *to proclaim the year of the* LORD*'s favor*
> *and the day of vengeance of our God,*
> *to comfort all who mourn . . .*
>
> (vv. 1-2)

Jesus defines the essentials of his mission. Nowhere in this passage do you see a mention of the Messiah coming to earth to save us for heaven.

Now, don't get me wrong; I believe in heaven, but not in the disembodied version portrayed in Greek philosophy. I believe in the biblical, redemptive re-creation of a new heavenly order that Jesus the Messiah initiated more than two thousand years ago. As described in Isaiah 61:4, the people of the messianic kingdom "will rebuild the ancient ruins and restore the places long devastated; they will renew the ruined cities that have been devastated for generations." Isaiah prophesies in the eighth century BCE that followers of the Messiah will not be sitting around passively waiting for his return, but will be actively preparing by rebuilding, restoring, and renewing broken people, systems, and societies. This passage, containing Jesus's mission statement, refers to the restoration of the broken and to the release of those who are bound and held captive. The gospel is good news for the poor, the oppressed, and the marginalized. And if it is not good news for the least of these, then it is not the gospel.

Also, understand that when *poverty* is used in the Bible, its meaning is broader than "economic limitation." Poverty, in the deepest biblical sense, is any kind of brokenness, whether that be in a personal or cultural context, that restricts people from living in the fullness of humanity that God intends.

Many of us born into the blessings of a first-world economy are blinded by our own spiritual poverty. Jesus warned the church at Laodicea about the spiritual poverty tied to their self-focused materialism: "So, because you are lukewarm—neither hot nor cold—I am about to spit you out of my mouth. You say, 'I am rich; I have acquired wealth and do not need a thing.' But you do not realize that you are wretched, pitiful, poor, blind and naked" (Revelation 3:16-17). We have often heard warnings against being lukewarm in our faith, of not being passionate or active. But we rarely talk about the second part of that passage: that the spiritual malaise we want to avoid is a direct result of our materialism.

Black Friday 2008 revealed the depth of the depravity of consumerist idolatry. A Long Island Walmart worker died after an out-of-control mob of frenzied shoppers smashed through the store's front doors and trampled him. Roughly two thousand people had gathered outside the doors in the predawn darkness. Chanting "Push the doors in!" the crowd pressed against the glass as the clock ticked down to the 5 a.m. opening. When it was time, the Black Friday stampede plunged the store into chaos, knocking employees to the ground and sending some shoppers scurrying on top of vending machines to avoid the danger. When the madness ended, thirty-four-year-old Jdimytai Damour was dead, and four shoppers, including a twenty-eight-year-old pregnant woman, had to be taken to the hospital. The police had to fight their way through the crowds to try to help the stricken man while people kept shopping.[1] Sadly, these shoving crowds of Black Friday represent the way in which far too many Americans, including many who claim to be followers of Jesus, herald the advent of his Christmas birth.

The coming of Jesus means that God is with us. Sometimes it is hard to see evidence of that, with all the sorrow and suffering in the world. Many people ask the question, "If God is all-loving and all-powerful, then why doesn't God do something about evil?" The answer to this question is simple: You are the "something" that God is sending to combat evil in this world. Evil will try to convince you that you can't change anything or really make a difference in this world. But, just as Jesus was sent by God to intervene in the world of evil, you were sent by Jesus, along with his power and resources, to bring light into dark places and to bring God's goodness where evil reigns.

You are the evidence that the Messiah of God's kingdom is present with us when what is broken around you is being restored, when the oppressed and captive are being set free, and when good news is being preached to the poor. Jesus's true followers are not just sitting together in religious meetings, passively waiting for his return. They are actively rebuilding the ancient ruins, restoring the places long devastated, and renewing ruined cities, devastated for generations (Isaiah 61:4). These are sacrificial values that run against the grain of our society's obsession with *Me! More! Bigger! Better!*

Everyone who recognizes Jesus as Messiah is a servant of his mission, and if that includes you and me, then we need to be committed to live more simply so that others may simply live—because that is what Jesus desires from his followers. The church, as the living body of Christ in the world, must act justly, love mercy, and walk humbly with God (Micah 6:8); love others as Jesus loves us (John 13:34-35); and make disciples of all nations (Matthew 28:18-20).

Let's Have a Real Birthday Bash!

Since gaining independence in 1956, Sudan has been a troubled land, plagued with civil war, genocide, poverty, and disease. I knew we had to do something big. I stood before our people in the fall of 2004 and said, "I want you to have a slim Christmas this year…and whatever you spend on your family, bring an equal amount for hunger relief in the Sudan. Because Christmas is not your birthday; it's Jesus's birthday." That Christmas, our people brought a Christmas miracle offering of more than $300,000.

We established a partnership with the United Methodist Committee on Relief (UMCOR) and laid the foundations for the Sudan Project (thesudanproject.org). The Sudan Project implemented a sustainable agriculture program in South Darfur. As a result, more than fifty-two hundred farming families were restocked with seed and supplies. Since then, the Sudan Project has implemented programs for child protection and development, safe access to clean water, and more. One hundred and seventy-nine new schools have provided safe havens and renewed hope for more than twenty-two thousand children, and life-skills training centers equip young men and women with marketable trades. Eighty-five thousand people have gained access to clean water. By mid-2011, Ginghamsburg Church, along with more than a hundred partner churches, schools, and businesses, had invested over $5 million (the final number was $8 million) in the Sudan Project.

Can you imagine the birthday celebration if every Christian in every church practiced the commitment of giving an equal amount of what they spend on themselves to a specific mission for Jesus somewhere in the world? We can change the world one place at a time, one person at a time, if we are willing to celebrate Jesus's birthday in a way that honors him. When we acknowledge Jesus as Lord, we give him the right to define our lifestyles, our values, and, yes, even the way we celebrate his birth. We do not exist for ourselves; we exist to be the hands and feet of Jesus in the world. If we are not doing that, we are not being the church.

At Christmas, we celebrate a messiah, a deliverer, who was born to die. So we, too, are called to give ourselves sacrificially with Christ for the world that God loves. More of him and less of us. More for him and less for us. Such sacrifice is paradoxical because the more of ourselves that we give away, the more abundant our faith and our contentment will be with what we have. In our culture of consumption, this is a countercultural way to live. Living on less when we could have more and giving away more when it means having less is a frightening proposition to many people. It is not easy, and there will be naysayers, but this sacrifice is what Jesus truly desires of those who would follow him.

An Alternative Celebration

Remember the e-mail I received from the person who didn't like our focus on Sudan each Christmas and was going to find a church more traditional to "the Christmas we know"?

Sometimes we worship tradition more than we worship Jesus, preferring the comfort of the familiar to the challenge and risk of doing something new. Honoring Jesus this Christmas may require the creation of some new traditions that are more focused on what Jesus wants from us than on what we desire for ourselves.

What are some of the alternative ways that you can identify for celebrating Jesus's birthday with family and friends this year?

One young adult cell group in our church found a creative way to raise money for Sudan in the months leading up to Christmas. Using a bar owned by the parents of one group member, they opened a restaurant to serve breakfast on Sunday mornings. They took several weeks to plan their hours, menu, and marketing, growing in faith and community as they organized and then staffed this temporary restaurant themselves. As a result, they raised more money than any of these young couples could have afforded to donate on their own.

The organizer of the event said this about the experience:

> I know for myself and my husband that, alone, we would not have followed through with the idea, but just as one of us would get discouraged somebody else in the group would get excited or find a new way to market the idea, and that would create momentum. At the end of October, for the next eight weeks, we opened up the restaurant every Sunday morning. Overall, we made around $3,000 for The Sudan Project. Each week we gained more supporters not only from the church but also from our community. In the end, our cell group grew greatly from the event. We learned how God blessed our trust that somebody would show up and that this call to action was really from him.

I hear stories like this one every year. There are small groups who serve together at a food pantry or clothing ministry. There are families who make things to sell or clear out the excess in their own homes and sell it. All to raise money for Sudan. Parents tend to think their children will be resistant to a plan that will mean fewer toys and gifts, but often the kids are the most enthusiastic about forming new traditions that help other people. There are even children who ask for donations to the Sudan Project rather than presents for themselves—not just on Jesus's birthday, but even on their own!

It doesn't have to be Sudan, of course. There are people in need all over the world and in our own cities—people whom Jesus loves and calls us to care for in his name. Other churches I know of have challenged their people to cut back on Christmas and give money instead to other international relief organizations or to local missions run by their own congregations. Some families buy fewer presents for themselves so that they can provide gifts to children who otherwise wouldn't receive anything or so they can sponsor a child all year long.

You can bet your bottom dollar that a gift like that will make Jesus smile on his birthday! How do I know? It comes down to this specific guidance: "Truly I tell you, whatever you did for one of the least of these brothers and sisters of mine, you did for me" and "whatever you did not do for one of the least of these, you did not do for me" (Matthew 25:40, 45). We serve Jesus by serving those in need. Simple as that.

It is so simple that when Jesus described the scene of the victorious king separating the sheep from the goats, he said many righteous people wouldn't even realize what they had done. Jesus said,

> *Then the righteous will answer him, "Lord, when did we see you hungry and feed you, or thirsty and give you something to drink? When did we see you a stranger and invite you in, or needing clothes and clothe you? When did we see you sick or in prison and go to visit you?"*
>
> *(Matthew 25:37-39)*

How funny that it can be so hard to find gifts that will please certain family members or friends—the people who seem to have everything—and yet it is so clear what the Lord of lords and King of kings wants for his birthday. God wants you—your time, your talent, and your treasure—used in service to others.

Questions for Reflection

- Are there people on your Christmas shopping list who are hard to shop for? What would happen if you put as much time and energy into Jesus's wish list each Christmas as you put into theirs?
- What big "buts" are keeping you from giving sacrificially? What excuses do you need to overcome to truly honor Jesus with your financial resources?
- Get creative! What new traditions and family practices could you start this year to make every Christmas a more authentic celebration of Jesus?

Chapter 5

BY A DIFFERENT ROAD

Chapter 5

BY A DIFFERENT ROAD

And they bowed down and worshiped him. Then they opened their treasures and presented him with gifts of gold, frankincense and myrrh. And having been warned in a dream not to go back to Herod, they returned to their country by another route.

(Matthew 2:11-12)

The holiday season of 2020 brought increased travel pressures due to the international travel restrictions caused by COVID-19. Domestic air travel saw plummeting demand, mandatory masks, blocked middle seats, and rigorous cleaning protocols. Traditional family travel plans and yearly celebrations abruptly had to change.

Needless to say, these days, flying can be frustrating, including arriving at the airport at least two hours early and waiting in long TSA lines. But I've learned you can reduce stress by paying special attention to how you pack. My mantra for travel is "less is more." If I can't fit what I need into a carry-on bag and a computer backpack, the surplus stays home. By carrying on, I save about one hour each round trip by not having to wait at baggage claim. That equates to twenty-four hours, or one whole day of my life, each year! The added assurance that my travel items will not be lost in the process also gives me peace of mind. I make sure my computer is readily accessible and that liquid and gel toiletries are in a clear, resealable one-quart bag before placing my carry-ons on the belt for inspection. Simplicity reduces stress—and that's an important principle not just for travel, and not just at Christmastime, but for all of life's endeavors.

The holiday season, which begins for many of us with Thanksgiving and continues through New Year's Day, often brings increased stress and even depression due to the dizzying demands and distractions of shopping, work parties, extended family visits, blended family responsibilities, cleaning, baking, entertaining, and—oh, yes—did I mention spending? To top it off, burning the candle at both ends makes us more susceptible to colds and other ailments.

Then we start off the new year with the guilt (and the inches) from overeating, the debt from overspending, and the emotional low that comes from the pursuit of fleeting joy. Meanwhile, the reason for the season—Immanuel, God with us—gets lost in the frantic complexity. But he doesn't have to.

After holiday vacations are over and the more organized among us have put the gifts and decorations away, we celebrate Epiphany—the arrival of the wise men or "magi" who came from afar to see the new king. Who were these mysterious magi who came to worship the infant Jesus? The true biblical account of the magi is an inspiring example of persistent, life-altering faith. Based on the information found in the Gospel of Matthew, Jesus would have been closer to the age of two when they arrived in Bethlehem. So while our decorative nativity sets place the magi next to the manger, the Gospel tells us they found Jesus much later and in a house, perhaps one that the family had rented or the home of a family friend. Many traditions have assumed that there were three magi, since they brought three specific gifts, but the biblical text does not number them. Later traditions began to add to the biblical story until, by the third century, they were viewed as kings. By the sixth century, they had names: Balthasar, Melchior, and Gaspar.

Further, in the real account, the energy and expense involved in their journey would have been considerable, given what appears to have been a two-year quest. And after the magi arrived at their destination, they offered Jesus treasures that would have been worthy only of a king.

We see in Matthew 2 the marks of true commitment:

- "They bowed down and worshiped him" (v. 11). When we acknowledge Jesus as Lord, we humbly submit to his authority. We acknowledge that he must have the defining rights in our lifestyles, values, and money. Remember, the worst kind of fool is the person who believes that God exists but lives as if God's directives are not to be taken seriously. There can be only one absolute authority in our lives. No longer God and Caesar or God and nation or God and partisan political party.

- "They opened their treasures" (v. 11). The resources of heaven do not fall from the sky; instead, they are released through God's people. God creates miracles through the resources that you and I hold in our hands. Miracles occur when we release our treasures to Jesus's hands for the purpose of multiplying God's redemptive work in the world.
- "They returned to their country by another route" (v. 12). Belief is simple, but changing course—or repenting and changing our life attitudes and practices—is often a hard commitment to make. When we acknowledge Jesus as Lord, however, we make that commitment to walk in new life directions—to travel by a different road. The biblical word for this kind of change in direction is *repentance.*

God's prophets have long been telling people to repent of their unjust, selfish ways. When John the Baptist saw many of the Pharisees and Sadducees coming out to where he was baptizing, he offered a rather provocative response: "You brood of vipers! Who warned you to flee from the coming wrath? Produce fruit in keeping with repentance" (Luke 3:7b-8a). When asked what they should do, John replied: "Anyone who has two shirts should share with the one who has none, and anyone who has food should do the same" (Luke 3:11). Likewise, for us, repenting of the self-focused ways of the world means embodying the countercultural values, priorities, and mission of Jesus on planet Earth.

January is a traditional time for many to commit to taking a different road. We see the New Year as a time for making resolutions, self-made promises to change something about our lives. Whether it be quitting a bad habit or starting smarter, healthier practices, we vow to make this year different.

It is interesting that while our calendar year starts in January, the traditional Christian calendar starts in late November, with Advent. So while the church is traditionally starting anew with the birth of Christ, most of us are winding down and taking stock of the past year. I'm not suggesting we move our New Year's Eve celebration back to November, but what if we allow the lessons of Advent and Christmas to shape the way we start the new calendar year—and the rest of our lives—by reorienting our priorities to focus not on ourselves but on the radical love Jesus gives to us and asks from us in return?

Right-Sizing Your Life for Mission

Jesus spoke about the subject of money and possessions more often than any other topic—even more than prayer and faith combined! We have to ask ourselves why this single subject is so important. Check your bank statement. Where does most of your money go? "For where your treasure is, there your heart will be also" (Matthew 6:21). Jesus is saying that our bank statement is the truest measure of the current state of our faith.

What we spend our money on reveals our ultimate values; it is a demonstration of what we truly worship. How we handle money is the window into our true character. Storing up treasures on earth without being rich toward God means that life is all about me, my family, and my family's needs and wants.

We then become disciples of the culture of consumption (self-focused) rather than disciples of the Lord Jesus (servant-focused). Overspending, debt, and attachment to material possessions hinder our ability to fully commit to following Jesus in sacrificial mission.

In the Gospel of Mark, we read about a man who sought Jesus out for the purpose of finding eternal life but then walked away when Jesus challenged his priorities. "'One thing you lack,' he said. 'Go, sell everything you have and give to the poor, and you will have treasure in heaven. Then come, follow me.' At this the man's face fell. He went away sad, because he had great wealth" (Mark 10:21-22). Quite simply, this man was too attached to his stuff to change his path and follow Jesus.

Jesus continually challenges our life values and priorities by making clear the contrast between the kingdom of God and the kingdom of consumption: "No one can serve two masters. Either you will hate the one and love the other, or you will be devoted to the one and despise the other. You cannot serve both God and money" (Matthew 6:24). You can't live with one foot in the kingdom of God and the other in the kingdom of consumption; the two represent radically opposing views about the meaning of life and the pursuit of happiness.

The market economy has a tremendous sway over our values and priorities, and the gospel message has been diluted with the materialistic focus that comes with the pursuit of the American dream. Victor Lebow, a leading post–World War II economist and retail analyst, defined the nature of the society we live in:

> Our enormously productive economy demands that we make consumption our way of life, that we convert the buying and use of goods into rituals, that we seek our spiritual satisfaction, our ego satisfaction in consumption. . . . We need things consumed, burned up, worn out, replaced, and discarded at an ever accelerating rate.[1]

Bigger houses, newer and nicer cars, ever larger and better flat-screen TVs, and dream vacations have led Americans into a black hole of consumer debt from which we may never fully recover. The size of the American family has shrunk over the last thirty years, but our homes have gotten 42 percent larger.[2] We eat out more and spend less time cooking, yet kitchen sizes have doubled. As Alan and Deb Hirsch have said,

> For most people in Western contexts, shopping is spirituality. It is an attempt to find meaning and happiness in the product. . . . Once again we are back to idolatry: the attempt to establish meaning and purpose on our own terms outside of a relationship with God—or as theologian Paul Tillich defined it, giving ultimate value to that which is not ultimate.[3]

We have forgotten the most fundamental priority of faith. We can't find life and meaning in things.

I must confess; I have been infected! I finally broke down and bought an iPhone 17 when my iPhone 10 still worked fine. My reasoning? I wanted the better camera. The consumer matrix system that we are born into has made consumption a primary addiction for many of us. Is it any wonder we are overstressed, depressed, and deeply in debt?

We need to remember that life is not about you and me. All of life's failures and detours come because of our own self-centered expectations and attachments. When we use God to get what we desire instead of being used by God for God's desire, we miss the opportunity to follow Immanuel, God with us. Jesus doesn't guarantee physical wealth and health in this life, and commitment to following Jesus isn't about safety and security. As a matter of fact, the promise is that "everyone who wants to live a godly life in Christ Jesus will be persecuted" (2 Timothy 3:12). But don't forget the words of the angel Gabriel to Mary: "Do not be afraid, Mary; you have found favor with God" (Luke 1:30). "'I am the Lord's servant,' Mary answered. 'May your word to me be fulfilled'" (Luke 1:38). And that is why we can respond: "I am your servant, Lord, regardless of what comes my way. Let it be done to me according to your will!"

The Kingdom of God as Priority

Jesus names the alternative life path for his followers:

> *So do not worry, saying, "What shall we eat?" or "What shall we drink?" or "What shall we wear?" For the pagans run after all these things, and your heavenly Father knows that you need them. But seek first his kingdom and his righteousness, and all these things will be given to you as well.*
>
> *(Matthew 6:31-33)*

What does Jesus mean when he talks about seeking first the kingdom of God? The kingdom of God is the place where God's invisible rule is made visible and the place where evidence of God's presence is demonstrated through a community of people living in submission to God's authority. The people of God become a living demonstration of heaven's priorities on earth. Heaven's resources are channeled through our obedience. This is what Jesus meant when he told his disciples,

> *Very truly I tell you, whoever believes in me will do the works I have been doing, and they will do even greater things than these, because I am going to the Father. And I will do whatever you ask in my name, so that the Father may be glorified in the Son. You may ask me for anything in my name, and I will do it.*
>
> *(John 14:12-14)*

The miracle of multiplication occurs because people living in pursuit of Jesus's kingdom priority make themselves completely available as wombs for God's blessings to the world.

There is a second directive for following Jesus's alternative life path: "Seek first [God's] kingdom and [God's] righteousness" (Matthew 6:33). *Righteousness* means "right acting in our relationships," or acting ethically in our relationships, both with God and with others. Acting ethically or rightly means actively working to promote and ensure God's redemptive purpose for all of God's children. Faith without works is dead! "If you know that [Jesus] is righteous, you know that everyone who does what is right has been born of him" (1 John 2:29). Did you catch the "does what is right" part? We distort the gospel when we reduce faith to having only right beliefs. You can't separate your actions toward God from your actions toward people.

The prophet Isaiah reminds us that our religious rituals mean nothing if not accompanied by righteous actions toward people:

> *"Is not this the kind of fasting I have chosen:*
> *to loose the chains of injustice*
> *and untie the cords of the yoke,*
> *to set the oppressed free*
> *and break every yoke?*
> *Is it not to share your food with the hungry*
> *and to provide the poor wanderer with shelter—*
> *when you see the naked, to clothe him,*
> *and not to turn away from your own flesh and blood?"*
> *(Isaiah 58:6-7)*

The prophet Amos used harsh words of disdain concerning the failure to equate faith with righteous practical actions:

> *"I hate, I despise your religious festivals;*
> *your assemblies are a stench to me.*
> *Even though you bring me burnt offerings and grain offerings,*
> *I will not accept them.*
> *Though you bring choice fellowship offerings,*
> *I will have no regard for them.*
> *Away with the noise of your songs!*
> *I will not listen to the music of your harps.*
> *But let justice roll on like a river,*
> *righteousness like a never-failing stream!"*
> *(Amos 5:21-24)*

Travel Light—Less Is More

Jesus sent his twelve disciples out with very specific directives, which included packing instructions for a mission lifestyle: "Do not get any gold or silver or copper to take with you in your belts—no bag for the journey or extra shirt or sandals or a staff, for the worker is worth his keep" (Matthew 10:9-10). In other words, don't allow your life to become overburdened with too much stuff and consumed by debt.

The A&E television series *Hoarders* brought Americans up close and personal with the obsessive-compulsive disorder of hoarding. Compulsive hoarding is the excessive acquisition of possessions. In each episode, we meet a person who has become estranged from their family and friends because of an addiction to collecting things, and many of the items collected are never used or discarded.

If we are honest with ourselves, there is a pack rat in all of us. Carolyn and I have been married for going on six decades, and it amazes me what we have collected in that time. For the first three decades of our marriage, I collected sports memorabilia (still do). Now, our basement looks like a sports bar/museum, complete with a pool table and a 1949 Coke machine. Before my parents moved from their home into a retirement community, my sister and I spent several weekends going through their stacks of boxes, which represented seven decades of their lives. I found so many treasures connected to childhood memories that I carried home four more boxes to add to our own growing collections. We have been talking about downsizing, but what will we do with all our stuff?

Jesus tells a parable about a man whose farming endeavors yielded an abundant harvest, presenting him with a rather promising dilemma: What would he do with the excess?

> *"This is what I'll do. I will tear down my barns and build bigger ones, and there I will store my surplus grain. And I'll say to myself, 'You have plenty of grain laid up for many years. Take life easy; eat, drink and be merry.'"*
>
> *But God said to him, "You fool! This very night your life will be demanded from you. Then who will get what you have prepared for yourself?"*
>
> *(Luke 12:18-20)*

Now catch Jesus's main point in this parable: "This is how it will be with whoever stores up things for themselves but is not rich toward God" (Luke 12:21). The more we have, the harder we have to work to maintain what we have, which means less time to develop relationships with those closest to our hearts and less time to serve Jesus's mission for the least and the lost. This is why Jesus challenges his disciples with the KISS principle—Keep It Simple, Saints. More isn't more. Less is more!

This fundamental principle of simplicity is also used in the design industry. For designers, simplicity should be a key goal, and unnecessary complexity should be avoided. When real estate stagers come into a home that has been difficult to sell, they declutter. After all, a space expands when not filled. Similarly, we need margins and open spaces in our lives if we want to make time for quality relationships, both with others and with God.

Carolyn and I have discovered the necessity of holding periodic garage sales not only to raise funds to fulfill God's mission but also to support the well-being of our souls. Our outward world is a reflection of our inner world: We have to clean up outer space to open up inner space as well as to release underused resources for God's mission.

What do you own that you never or rarely use that is taking up space? One of the simple ways that I plan to declutter this Christmas is to clean out my overstuffed coat closet. I have numerous nice coats and leather jackets, many that I haven't worn in years. Do you have any winter coats in your closet that you rarely wear? Why not give them to folks who really need them this winter?

Making Life Different

Let me suggest the following three practices to reorient your life in the New Year so that you can experience the joy of living and giving like Jesus:

- Proactive parenting
- Practical service
- Sharing the good news

Proactive Parenting

In a me-focused culture with ill-defined moral values, proactive parenting requires patience and persistence. Parenting comes with huge amounts of responsibility and trust. Have you ever wondered why God entrusted Joseph with the responsibility of being Jesus's earthly father and role model? We are not given much information about Joseph's background. He must have been a man of few words, since he isn't quoted even once in the four Gospels. We know that Joseph came from a common background and made his living as a carpenter, possibly a furniture maker or stonemason. It has been assumed that Joseph was older and died sometime between Jesus's early teen years and the beginning of his public ministry. Joseph is not mentioned after the birth narratives except on one occasion—the family's annual pilgrimage to Jerusalem for the Feast of Passover, when Jesus was twelve. Some extrabiblical sources refer to Joseph having been previously married, from which Jesus's brothers and sisters came.

We don't know much about Joseph, but we are told that he possessed one very significant character trait: compassion. After the emotional shock of discovering what he believed to be his fiancée's betrayal, he responded with compassion. "Because Joseph her husband was faithful to the law, and yet did not want to expose her to public disgrace, he had in mind to divorce her quietly" (Matthew 1:19). Joseph was a righteous man. He was a person who would act on the basis of Scriptural principles and God's directives, regardless of his emotional state or adverse circumstances.

God chose Abraham for a similar reason. "For I have chosen him, so that he will direct his children and his household after him to keep the way of the LORD by doing what is right and just, so that the Lord will bring about for Abraham what he has promised him" (Genesis 18:19).

Parenting is a task trusted to us by God. You and I are given the responsibility to be the light bearers for our children—that is, to light the way of Immanuel, God with us. The Torah warns us to be righteous so that our children can follow our example: "Only be careful, and watch yourselves closely so that you do not forget the things your eyes have seen or let them fade from your heart as long as you live. Teach them to your children and to their children after them" (Deuteronomy 4:9). True faith is both taught and caught (modeled) through the generations. The Apostle Paul reminded his young protégé, Timothy: "I am reminded of your sincere faith, which first lived in your grandmother Lois and in your mother Eunice and, I am persuaded, now lives in you also" (2 Timothy 1:5).

Let's show our children how to serve God's purpose by helping others rather than being self-focused consumers of Santa Claus marketing. After all, life is all about relationships.

How can you spend less time making and spending money and more time being with those you love? If you find a way, your children will not only notice the changes but also benefit from them.

Practical Service Demonstrated Through Good Deeds

Jesus gives his followers a very clear directive for the promotion of his kingdom mission: "A new command I give you: Love one another. As I have loved you, so you must love one another. By this everyone will know that you are my disciples, if you love one another" (John 13:34-35).

People do not believe the gospel simply because of our words; seeing is believing. Our walk must precede our talk. "In the same way, let your light shine before others, that they may see your good deeds and glorify your Father in heaven" (Matthew 5:16). There is a quote (commonly misattributed to St. Francis of Assisi) that is so right on the mark: "Preach the Gospel at all times and, if necessary, use words."

Carolyn and I had some really good friends over to our home recently, just to enjoy each other's company. One of these friends, who is Jewish, asked me an important question that evening, which I continue to ask myself: "Mike, what's wrong with Christians? They don't even follow Jesus's teachings." Later that evening, I remarked to Carolyn what a difference it would make if Christians truly followed Jesus and not just worshiped Jesus.

Eighty-seven times in the Gospels, Jesus says, "Follow me," and zero times does he say, "Worship me." Yet so many of us put the emphasis on the zero. Churches measure success by the number of people in worship. Jesus didn't pray to raise up worshipers. He prayed to raise up workers (Matthew 9:37-38).

Previously, through New Path (our outreach ministry), we provided Christmas gifts to families in need through what we called the Adopt-a-Family program. While some of the program participants had positive experiences, others had experiences that made it difficult for them to experience wholeness. First, there was an inconsistency in the gift-giving. Second, some recipient parents felt embarrassed at not being able to provide even simple gifts for their children while watching perfect strangers bring them numerous items. The process sent a subtle message to parents of their inability to provide for their own children, so while it was a "warm fuzzy" experience for those giving, it became a stumbling block for those we were trying to help.

Sherry's story is a great example of a better way to offer support. Sherry was a single mom who had suffered through domestic violence and had been forced to flee her home, with her children, to find safety in emergency housing. After several months, she and her children found themselves without any resources at Christmas and with little hope of being able to even share a meal on the day. Rather than simply providing charity in a one-time gift, one church family developed an ongoing relationship with Sherry and her children that, in the end, was more valuable than presents under the tree. Sherry's life was changed because she felt accepted for who she was, regardless of what her family had been through. Her transformation was the result not of presents magically appearing under the tree but of relationships with brothers and sisters in Christ all year round. Sherry is now a program coordinator for our outreach ministries and is giving of herself daily to serve others. Her story taught us an important truth: Christmas is about developing lasting relationships with persons in poverty and not just about giving presents.

From that point on, our Christmas ministry took on a different look. We became intentional about sharing the story of Jesus's birth and the meaning of an intentional relationship with Jesus Christ. We now provide a "Christmas Shoppe," where parents can come and choose new toys and gifts for their children at no cost. But most important, we provide a full, four-course dinner, complete with candles, tablecloths, and live music, where our guest families are waited on by our church family. During this time, relationships are formed, and the church becomes a living example of what it means to serve and truly give of ourselves at Christmas. In addition, everyone involved becomes a part of the community, and respect and dignity are restored.

Another story is that of a young single mother who was undergoing treatment for cancer and was in a state of depression because of her medical situation and resulting poverty. She came to New Path to take a class and was led to our car ministry, through which she could earn a car by learning and serving. She was encouraged to serve by helping with preparations for the Christmas dinner and, in doing so, became connected with other servants. The experience gave her a new community—the body of Christ—and allowed her to be a part of the whole process of serving rather than a mere bystander attending an event. This woman's outlook is much different now because she knows the sacrifice of time and resources that is needed to "serve the least of these." Likewise, we, as the body of Christ, are changed because we see the transformative power of Jesus Christ at work through relationship and through those who have been served, who in turn become servants to others.

There are opportunities everywhere to be Christ's light by serving others' needs in practical ways. What is your church already doing? How can your family take an active role? What initiative can you bring to your faith community for participating in ministry with the poor? Remember, miracles begin with a simple act.

Sharing the Good News!

We need to go beyond just doing good deeds. We need to name the name and tell others the good news about Jesus. Can you imagine how awful it would be if you allowed me to see some incredible power at work in your life and then never shared its source? My life has been changed forever because of faithful people who lived the good news and then named the name that is above every name: Jesus Christ!

The Apostle Peter would never have met Jesus without the witness of his brother, Andrew. After Andrew's encounter with Jesus, he ran to tell his brother Peter, "We have found the Messiah" (John 1:41), after which Andrew took Peter to see Jesus in person.

This is what witnessing is all about: show (good deeds) and then tell (the reason). You don't have to try to convince anyone; leave that work to the Holy Spirit. And you don't have to shove Jesus down anyone's throat. Jesus himself was not self-aggrandizing when people asked about his significance and power. When John the Baptist sent his disciples to ask Jesus if he was "the one who was to come," Jesus replied, "Go back and report to John what you hear and see: The blind receive sight, the lame walk, those who have leprosy are cleansed, the deaf hear, the dead are raised, and the good news is proclaimed to the poor" (Matthew 11:3-5).

Sometimes people will ask me a question about faith that I don't have an answer for. I simply say, "I don't know. But come and see the way Jesus is transforming my life and the lives of others." God will do the rest!

Let Your Light Shine

I found myself one evening just sitting by the fire, taking in the Christmas tree, intermittently reading the first and second chapters of Matthew. I thought about how Christians had adopted the practice of decorating the evergreen tree as a symbol of eternal life—a reminder to stay focused on things eternal. The tannenbaum (fir tree) was the only tree that didn't seem to die during the winter. It stayed ever green.

Likewise, long before Christians adopted the winter solstice as the time in which they would celebrate Jesus's birth, candles were used to signify Christ as the light of the world. In medieval times, before the Santa legend, Christians would place candles in their windows to welcome the Christ Child, who was looking for places where he would be invited in. No one knew for sure how he might appear. Perhaps he would come dressed in the rags of a beggar, or he might come as a poor and lonely child. Maybe he would come in the form of a person with disabilities or as a homeless wanderer of the streets. It became customary for devout Christians to welcome into their homes any of "the least of these" who knocked at their doors on Christmas Eve. To turn away anyone might have meant the rejection of the Christ Child, who had come in unfamiliar garb.

They realized that the Christmas season is a great time to focus on life priorities that really matter: faith, family, friends, service. Now, the reason for the season can get lost in frantic preparation and forgotten once the tree is taken down. But it doesn't have to.

We are called at Christmas and all year through to look for and serve Jesus in the homeless who wander the streets, in the children infected with HIV, and in the refugees affected by senseless war and other tragedies. We can let the light of Christ shine in our lives through the love we show to others.

Put a candle in your window to welcome the lost and lonely—and to welcome Jesus himself.

Questions for Reflection

- How can you simplify your home to create more room for peace and togetherness, rather than for more stuff? What excess can you get rid of in your home (or your schedule!) to more accurately reflect where your priorities lie?
- What would it mean for you to "seek God's kingdom first"? What changes would that shift necessitate in your life?
- Take a moment right now to think of ways you can make first things first in the New Year by finishing the following sentences:
    - ◊ I will spend more time with the people I love by ________________________________.
    - ◊ I will demonstrate my faith in practical service by ________________________.
    - ◊ I will cultivate my relationship with God by ________________________________.

NOTES

Introduction

1 "Consumers to Spend Second-Highest Amount on Record, According to NRF Holiday Survey," National Retail Federation, October 16, 2025, https://nrf.com/media-center/press-releases/consumers-to-spend-second-highest-amount-on-record-according-to-nrf-holiday-survey.

2 Zina Kumok, "Average Credit Card Debt by U.S. Household in 2026," CardRates.com, July 2, 2025, https://www.cardrates.com/advice/average-credit-card-debt-by-us-household/.

1. Expect a Miracle

1 Quoted in Rueben Job and Norman Shawchuck, *A Guide to Prayer for Ministers and Other Servants* (The Upper Room, 1983), 250.

2 Alan Hirsch and Debra Hirsch, *Untamed: Reactivating a Missional Form of Discipleship* (Baker Books, 2010), 137.

2. Giving Up on Perfect

1 Reggie McNeal, *The Present Future: Six Tough Questions for the Church* (Jossey-Bass, 2003), 1.

2 Quoted in David Van Biema, "Mother Teresa's Crisis of Faith," *Time*, August 2007. https://time.com/4126238/mother-teresas-crisis-of-faith/.

3. Scandalous Love

1 "8 Important Facts About World Hunger," International Relief Committee, August 15, 2026, https://www.rescue.org/article/eight-hunger-facts.

2 Visit https://beatmalaria.org/ for more statistics and to donate nets.

3 “Sudan Wins a Key African Award for Hygiene and Sanitation,” UNICEF, November 12, 2009, https://reliefweb.int/report/sudan/sudan-wins-key-african-award-hygiene-and-sanitation.

4. Jesus’s Wish List

1 Ken Belson and Karen Zraick, “Mourning a Good Friend, and Trying to Make Sense out of a Stampede,” *New York Times*, November 30, 2008, https://www.nytimes.com/2008/11/30/nyregion/30walmart.html.

5. By a Different Road

1 Victor Lebow, “Price Competition in 1955,” *Journal of Retailing*, Spring 1955, https://mronline.org/wp-content/uploads/2019/07/Lebow.pdf.

2 James R. Barth, Tong Li, and Rick Palacios Jr., “McMansion Economics,” *Los Angeles Times*, November 21, 2010, http://articles.latimes.com/2010/nov/21/opinion/la-oe-barth-big-houses-20101121.

3 Hirsch and Hirsch, *Untamed*, 118–119.